BNP

Best NEW Poets

2020

50 Poems from Emerging Writers

Guest Editor Brian Teare

Series Editor Jeb Livingood

This book is published in cooperation with *Meridian* (readmeridian.org) and the University of Virginia Press (upress.virginia.edu).

For additional information, visit us at
bestnewpoets.org
twitter.com/BestNewPoets
facebook.com/BestNewPoets

Cover design by 4 Eyes Design, 4eyesdesign.com

Text set in Adobe Garamond Pro and Bodoni

Printed by Bailey Printing, Charlottesville, Virginia

ISBN: 978-0997562347
ISSN: 1554-7019

Contents

About *Best New Poets*

Welcome to *Best New Poets 2020*, our sixteenth annual anthology of fifty poems from emerging writers. In *Best New Poets*, the term "emerging writer" is defined narrowly: we restrict our anthology to poets who have yet to publish a book-length collection of poetry. Our goal is to provide special encouragement and recognition to poets just starting in their careers, the many writing programs they attend, and the magazines that publish their work.

From February to May of 2020, *Best New Poets* accepted nominations from writing programs and magazines in the United States and Canada. Each magazine and program could nominate two writers, and those poets could send a free submission to the anthology. For a small entry fee, writers who had not received nominations could also submit poems as part of our open competition. Eligible poems were either published after January 1, 2019, or unpublished. Which means you are not only reading new poets in this book, but also some of their most recent work.

In all, we received over 2,200 submissions for a total of nearly 4,000 poems. A pool of readers and the series editor ranked these submissions, sending a few hundred selections to this year's guest editor, Brian Teare, who chose the final fifty poems that appear here.

Cintia Santana
REIGN

which is to say in december's early darkness which is to say in a horseshoe bat, unbothered
after thousands of years which is to say in a pig, a pangolin, a palm civet, a wet market in
Guangdong, perhaps a hybrid by then, in seven days risen from 200 to 13,000, zoonotic, spokes
like keys to latch onto lungs, sightless, which is to say—what can be said?—of the dying dying
alone, untouched—each one ours and countless—shuttered, people and places which is to say
hunger set in, and hunger for skin, for crowd-hum which is to say the tulip magnolia blossomed,
spent, and the weeping cherry's crown grew studded by pale pink butterflies which is to say the
black phoebe, the rock wren, the dark-eyed junco, gathered, strand by strand, a dog's stray fur,
a bright bit of hay which is to say the mate darted nearby, down from the camellia, the branch
then swinging which is to say the flower, ripe, petticoated, bounced in the wild april air before
hitting ground which is to say spring, somehow, and what the virus did was seek to live

Jameka Williams
My Sister Says [Everyone Can Catch This Smoke]

A bullet disappears inside a man's chest
faster than a hand clears smoke
from the end of a cigarette.

Penn & Teller perform a magic trick,
More accurately, an illusion: mute Teller shoots
verbose Penn in the mouth with a handgun.

Penn smiles. Clenched between his teeth: a gold bullet.
Its butt caved by the hammer, but otherwise clean, glinting.
Penn, for the record, does not believe in miracles.

["The depressed person is a radical, sullen atheist."]
But like Christ, Penn & Teller perform anti-death.
Some kind of gods.

A gun is a magic wand.
So when my sister says she will hunt the man who pushed me into the
concrete ████████████████████████ she has a trick up her sleeve.

████████ my sister says ██████ hunt the man ████████████████
████████████████████████ she ████████████████████

Merriam-Webster:
i.   To pursue—
ii.   To pursue *with intent to capture*
iii.   To traverse *in search of prey*

*

[inside you will find me eating entire black suns.

████████████████████████████ man ████████ me in ██████
concrete ██ parking garage & ████████████████████████
██████

So when my sister says she will hunt the man who pushed me in ██████
concrete ████████████████ me ████████████████████████
██████

     a black sun.   inside.
     you will find.   a black sun.   split me.]

                 *

[Kristeva: "Naming suffering, exalting it, dissecting it into its smallest components—that is doubtless a way to curb mourning."]

When my sister says she will
traverse
intent to
capture
prey

             [who split me]
I have to make-believe she will.

A gun is a magic   [I do not believe in spells & incantations].

A sullen atheist, I enjoy
the language of violence.
The way it bounces
across my tongue,

between my teeth.
The rhetoric of vengeance
                    [& the Lord shall have It]
in the female mouth
can be unctuous.

Revenge fantasy:
Teeth clenched down
on an Adam's apple.
My teeth clean, glinting.

But, of course, there is no God.
                              I blink the illusion of death away.

                    *

My sister & I are in
Walmart shopping
for pistols. Our black
pupils bright with
swelling conviction.

She grips a gun
as easy as holding
a flat iron to her scalp.

"Tell me what
he looks like,"
she'll say.

I say: [Everyone.]

Threa Almontaser
Hidden Bombs in My Coochie

١

my accent not arab enough
to haggle   people know I'm not native
from my swaying
flux   in the city   rundown brick-slabs
the lost nipping your heels
for a soft touch
an outlaw asks where home is
finds it funny when I say *demi yemeni*
I board the plane back
to my birthplace   sturdy
blue proof in my pocket
alien again when I land

٢

I sing two anthems
hold a moshed lineage
in every boxed foyer
I walk   baba still speaks to me
in arabic   but we listen
to britney spears   watch family feud
remind ourselves of yemen
with the kubz as utensil
when we kiss cheeks
in odd numbers   remember
a grove's perfuming
before the marooned onslaught
when children didn't play

the game with charcoal & cotton
called   who can make
gasmasks the fastest

٣

when I step outside
violence becomes a rising
of my neck hairs   running
through a murky two-lane
out of breath so I don't end up
like bambi's mama shot dead
in my tracks   I can't say
I never saw it coming
curled fetal in a forest
caucasian man's bullet in this
dumb blah-brain my small son
waiting in a tree's shadow for me
to surge up from the tall grass
nudge his wet dark nose
with my nose

٤

in america I am automatic:
towelhead & hidden
bombs in my coochie
ass fat for that isis
dick 9/11 suss-lookin'
bitch that sandy-toed
camel fucker cousin fucking
to make more terrorist
babies a fourth wife
mia khalifa in a burkha
lookin' bitch long rifle

nose from your uncle
bin laden lil' bitch

◦

amreeka settles my body
into place   it unbends
the flick of my wrists
when I talk   turns
my femurs into fire escapes
eyes canonized chasms
my neck's axis craning
down   it tells baristas
my name is tina
tongue ebbing far away
from me
the news makes me believe
I was born to cock
back this rifle sleek & steady
like a true terrorist the news
makes me want to grab
my phone & gun
it out the country
the news makes me touch
myself   find the panic
button of my body
& press hard

—Nominated by *Passages North*

Jai Dulani
My Name

1.

I am in a bazaar with my mom,
meat slices hang like earrings.
she shakes her head, clucking, *it's too expensive*

> when I wanted to come out to extended family
> she warned   *they   are   not   worth   it.*
> bizarre. the cost of nourishment.

2.

chunni covered head, backlit woman leans
in, says *we met in 1976.* I told her *I wasn't born
yet. Must be mistaken.* The impossibility
of knowing me, squints. Scrunch sun stain.

> new country, who dis?
>   no brief explanation of this body.
> do we all land, sweetly, here?

3.

parallel park this. blue steel colossal truck.
is it possible? to be here? passing light blares.
unwieldly maneuvering. Precious, keep driving.

Narrow family space   Rearview glare
tears my eyes.

4.

truck full of goods.
what we owe/ what we have
left after getting what/ we wanted.

protect them? protect
me? the shell broke.
Jai   means   *victory   to*

5.

I am at a long table. A writer stands up, she
gives someone a piece of her mind. Her curly hair
swishes, her finger points.

What if I was talking, like it mattered?

Kathleen Balma
Lap Dance with No Ending

There's a bouncer in this poem, watching
you read it. His name is Vic. Vic won't make
eye contact, won't bug you unless I signal
distress. I've never had to do that in poetry
yet. He was in the army. Discreet as a landmine.
So long as you keep still and do nothing
while I work, he won't interrupt this lit
experience. Vic may or may not have killed.
He may or may not use meth. He *does* work out.
He *does* know my routine. He's seen me do it
dozens of nights. He knows all the words
to the money songs. His peripheral vision
is muscular. It sees every crook and swerve
of me, though he and I don't speak and I
have never touched him. It's crucial that you
fear him while my naked's in your face.
Only sometimes you need more. The dog
tags looped through my shoe strap, those
aren't Vic's. I can defuse a bomb with my teeth.

Tasia Trevino
The Other Side of Mt. Heart Attack

A VISIT FROM DRUM

the first time I get double-bass beats it's two hours the nurses take my pressure tell me don't stand wheel me in a chair to a bed Mom cowers in the corner by the crash cart they tear off my clothes attach leads ready a 16-gauge needle the doctor says this isn't going to feel good a feeling floods my right arm my body seizes I sit up they push me back on the bed they do it again my beats relax the EMT says that works nine times out of ten and the other time I ask

if I keep count I could control this expensive somersault phantom several false starts no money for follow-up is it fatal or just a condition without coverage I develop distractions codependence on the strength of strings learn to sing at house shows with shitty PAs strain against the squall for years no one can hear me just the Boys on guitar bass and drums turn my back to the crowd when I sing over stimulated vagus I can't stop performing wish for some assurance I'm going to make it

Los Angeles seeped into my bloodlines when Dad stick-and-poked Mom a fleur-de-lis on her ankle while watching *The Decline of Western Civ* Vol. 1 twenty years later I move to the city in an ancient Buick I dream to be Jeffrey Lee Sable Starr a sea bird over light-dotted hills the observatory's formal white gown feel for my pulse during sound check the Boys ask me what language are my lyrics Persephone I say Eurydice rock myself to sleep in double-time cross my heart hope to know which feeling I'm faking

BE QUIET MT. HEART ATTACK!

I stop taking off my hospital bracelet I don't have insurance so I can't afford to know why I have some ideas but the Boys keep saying "you're fine you're fine" swatting my fingers from the right side of my neck me swallowing blues to keep myself at bay am I still their Wendy Bird they were there all the times they stopped my heart maybe the reason for it too I ping-pong the aisles at the Last Bookstore wait for the calm to kick in search out every iteration of sunset

on stage singing grief for each of my past selves in a room sparse with solitary men most nights I dull my pounding with tequila rocks lime another round with the Boys and the Gretsch never get paid to play drag myself home on unlit side streets past box-top shrines stuffed with sweets and sticky rice in a dream I carry one of the Boys on my back through the Hollywood Farmers' Market I buy peonies and small cabbages this is this not a dream this is

I gather the handwritten receipts from the mechanic they make a $3,000 pile still my Buick bucks stalls it has no AC or heat no defrost have to roll down the windows in a storm the armrest gets streaked with grime drive out to Altadena for a job get $10/hr to survey places people want to film I size up other drivers wonder how they afford it I want my ass sliding on leather interior I want to see the inside of a stranger's house wonder whether I'll ever move

DRUM GETS A GLIMPSE

when I'm not onstage I get a job selling things I can't understand to people I never see I finally go to the doctor he says I'm fine I just have anxiety need to eat more fiber he gives me a non-refillable prescription for Ativan and suppositories tells me buy Metamucil drink that every day I get regular lose a lot of memories start to need a bigger audience almost fight the bouncer after karaoke at the Blue Goose put the tinsel Xmas tree up with no gifts underneath

my boss is a Scorp/Sag cusp he wears tennis shoes nice jeans floral dress shirt top two buttons undone at the Xmas party he puts his hand btwn my legs when he bends down to kiss me hello brings me into his office for my three-month review says he wants to give me a raise thinks I'm smart but not showing it seems like I don't care I make hourly as much as his maids he tells me they're stupid always putting things in the wrong place he tells me earn my raise

Tuesday afternoon I have a panic attack at an impromptu audition for a reality series that's shooting upstairs from my office they like me for the part of expert on a show about aliens visiting Earth I take a Valium walk around the block go to urgent care the nurse slaps adhesive electrodes to my chest unshaven shins she won't give me Xanax she says I need a cardiologist when I tell her about the first time how they had to stop my heart

LET'S NOT WRESTLE MT. HEART ATTACK

it's a catheter-based procedure they'll make a slit in my leg thread a wire up my vein into my heart they'll jack up my heart rate until the bad rhythm kicks in they'll burn those pathways closed I'll be sedated not asleep I'll go home the same day never think about it again there are risks perforation stroke I lose my insurance in a week I say how soon can we do it how about in three days the doctor says I shake her hand and ask for one day off work

my first surgery is the day before Thanksgiving I don't want Mom or Dad to come but they do in preop two nurses dry-shave my groin joke about filming me talking candid in twilight sleep Dad gets ramen downtown after I'm fine everyone leaves I stain the hospital bed with blood the nurse changes my tampon I go home the same day the next day the Boys come over we drink Wild Turkey and I cook everyone proper dinner with pressure dressing

I can't leave the city bc my Buick shuts off at every stoplight the record label with interest wants more demos I'm going to write a song a day so far I haven't written one in months the only constants are always late with rent for the practice space phone bill groceries and fights I don't remember picking up the Gretsch dampen its strings when someone walks by the Buick catches fire on the 5 the mechanic cuts out the catalytic converter puts in a pipe I keep driving

TO HOLD YOU, DRUM

on my lunch break I talk to the head of the label he has me on speakerphone sitting on a marble memorial bench in Hollywood Forever pretending I can understand everything he says he has to say something to me he doesn't want to be the stereotypical record label guy but he can't pronounce all of our song names he loves frontwomen female drummers we talk for thirty-six minutes he says he will be out in LA later this month we should meet for coffee I wonder if he doesn't drink

I can't stop thinking about my heart my windowless office I get an hour off work to see a social worker at Kaiser she says I had no guidance I've been drinking that much since I was sixteen I should stop playing music it seems too stressful go back to grad school get into debt like everyone else she doesn't know what I can do with a degree in history I pick a handful of night jasmine on my walk home the only things I think about more than my heart are money the dying car how I don't feel

the farthest I can run in the city is Teardrop Park where the view is El Chubasco Chinatown and a city disguised my body buzzes badly with want my heart leans out of tempo sometimes it's inhalation sets it off sometimes the weather not enough water sometimes too much food not enough sometimes it's being in bed with someone being in bed alone it's extra beats an electrical problem not something I control what's the chorus again

YOU, DRUM

on Lou Reed's birthday I watch porn on my phone in the bathroom
before dinner with the Boys we bring our own booze I start to cry about
Caetano Veloso in exile signing in English I walk home a man jerks off in
a bush outside the corner liquor store eyes rolled back furious pumping I
pass Jumbo's where we went with the Boys for my twenty-first birthday
me sitting close to the stage them sitting against the wall in the shadows
beckoning me with dollar bills to give to the girls

Tuesdays are band practice Wednesdays are all night happy hour the
bartendress with huge eyes and French braids makes me at least three tequila
sodas I think about her naked sit outside on year-round-bougainvillea-
shaded patio papier mâché petals spiked vines I dim the lights in the bar's
pink bathroom take a picture of myself wish for someone to send it to
walk home under graying skies one of the men outside 7-Eleven calls to
me hey sloppy girl asks me for a blowjob

I need another surgery it's forty-thousand dollars but it's covered if I keep
my job Mom comes and Gramma but Dad already had tickets to see John
Doe only Mom has a panic attack on my futon so I drive us to Kaiser
across the street from the big blue church that took all of Gramma's
money she holds my hand the nurses mistake her for my mom and me for
nineteen I'm awake again during the doctor says he found the problem he
says my heart tricked them last time

IT'S ALL BLOOMING NOW MT. HEART ATTACK

sometimes I think I like Los Angeles I go downtown to see television
with the Boys walk through a heist scene that doesn't stop rolling Tom
Verlaine gestures to Venus in the western sky I'm in love with all my
friends climax in the shower to Roy Orbison falling I'm falling falling in
love with heartbeat throb dream one of the Boys has me in public press
the wooden spoon handle against myself in my galley kitchen while the
rice cooks on the stove

the label doesn't want to sign us I get weepy at the bar with the Boys I
let down my love for the city but I only know one kind it's killing me
sometimes I feel very sad I tell the Boys that the same session band played
on every American pop hit of the sixties no one knows their names I start
to lose momentum trust practice sincerity in the bathroom mirror ask for
my memories back erased or otherwise find myself among scattered palm
fronds and street roaches on the edge of Santa Monica

the doctor says another surgery would risk perforation my heart has two
pacemakers sometimes the false one gets the rhythm the real one gets a
break after I leave the city I can't stop dancing at the least appropriate
times I come back to the city but don't make it past Mulholland I stand
on a borrowed balcony over behind-the-scenes streets without sidewalks
so close to all my landmarks I can taste lemongrass tripas and tarna can see
my beating the score is swelling

THE OTHER SIDE OF MT. HEART ATTACK

there is no way to see a city I can't be anymore at the junction of thickly-traveled boulevards a city invariably comes into existence I dream washing machine amps rubbery guitar strings mics with no input I let myself go slack the tempo evens out I wear the skinniest tuxedo I can find put on lipstick in the hospital bed I allow a place to tame me a heavy quiet settles around me I don't know what to do with it don't know how to allow myself this pace worry where will my voice be if not a stage

CONSIDER!
DIFFERENT!
FADING!
SYSTEMS!

grief for me for the part on a dream for somersault phantom sparse with sweets and drums CONSIDER! DIFFERENT! FADING! SYSTEMS! turn my past selves into a chair into a bed they tear off my past selves in a dream I can't stop drinking that's shooting upstairs from my Tuesday afternoon I have a panic attach leads reality series that's shooting in my heart CONSIDER! DIFFERENT! FADING! SYSTEMS! are risks perforation stroke I lose pathways clothes attack to grad school get into debt like Xanax CONSIDER! DIFFERENT! FADING! SYSTEMS! closed I'll burn those pathways I'll be sedated I'll go home the stereotypical record label against my body seizes my beats relax the label has me for one of the Boys on my back CONSIDER! DIFFERENT! FADING! SYSTEMS! he doesn't want to be again in Hollywood Forever pretending he loves from my body CONSIDER! DIFFERENT! FADING! SYSTEMS! when I sit up they tear off my time I tell her hand and ask for a condition with sweets stuffed with the Boys most nights CONSIDER! DIFFERENT! FADING! SYSTEMS! my clothes attack at an impromptu audition stroke I lose my insurance and they do it can we do it how about they do it CONSIDER! DIFFERENT! FADING! SYSTEMS! fatal or just the Boys on my lunch break I think to my unshaven shitty codependence on the bed I've been

drinking about aliens visiting Earth I think about LA later another handful
go back stressful go back through the Hollywood Farmers' Market for
years no one can say how soon can we be the Gretsch never time how
soon can we talk to grad school get double-bass beats ready a 16-guage
needle they'll make me a slit in a week I say CONSIDER! DIFFERENT!
FADING! SYSTEMS! some assurance I've been drinking never anything
never false stage singing grief CONSIDER! DIFFERENT! FADING!
SYSTEMS! never false stage singing grief CONSIDER! DIFFERENT!
FADING! SYSTEMS! never false stage singing grief
never false stage singing grief
never false stage singing grief
never false
never false never false
oh you drum
oh you drum
my drum
my drum
my drum

This poem contains lyrics/references from *Drum's Not Dead* by the Liars, "Falling" by
Roy Orbison, "I Just Wasn't Made for These Times" by the Beach Boys, "The Strength of
Strings" by Gene Clark, and Brian Eno and Peter Schmidt's Oblique Strategies card deck.

Benjamin Garcia
Huitlacoche

Go ahead and call me what I am,
                  call me: faggot, homo, joto, pinche puto.
Unhusk me if you must, call me
                  acquired, call me dirty, call me corn smut.

      Though it looks like a prostate rolled in soot, huitlacoche
                  at the farmer's market sells as Mexican Truffle.
Yet farmers in your heartland treat it like a sickness.
                  And because disease can decimate a monoculture,

      they are afraid. That's why they bundle and they burn it,
                  a literal faggot. I said it and I'll say it.
Call me what I am, and if you can't pronounce
                  my surname, I'm supposed to say don't sweat it.

      Don't sweat it, because even huitlacoche is a corruption
                  of the Nahuatl cuitlacochin, which is a corruption
of cuitlacochi. Tongues make mistakes
                  and mistakes

      make languages. Like I was saying, for a long time
                  I couldn't pronounce them either, the things I like.
As with any delicacy, it's best
                  to start slow. Sound it out. Huit—

      la—co—che, an—u—lin—gus, mas—
                  tur—ba—tion. When you master
saying them out loud, it's time to rub any two
                  syllables together: cock, suck; pussy, fuck; ass, lick.

Relax. They are only words. They are the only words
                 you need to insult someone
or to have sex with them
                 no matter what country you find yourself in.

Words have their luggage like immigrants
                 have their customs. Huitlacoche, mariposa, maricón.
Now that I have put it in my mouth,
                 I am proud to be a faggot.

But it sounds so hateful when you say it.
                 A coworker really said this to me, I said
because that's the way I always heard it.
                 How do you speak such good English anyway?

Smile—say nothing—don't sweat it—he aimed it as a compliment.
                 Faggot, wetback, huitlacoche, all my life I've heard it.
Learning English, *it hurted* is what I would say
                 when I wanted to say *it hurt.* Not anymore. I know

all about tense agreement, just tell me where to conjugate
                 and I will. Shut your mouth—when I'm talking
spores come out in droves like mosquitos
                 birthed for blood—or I'll give you what I got.

Jasmine An
Sports Science

>   *—for B.A.*

the human is the hand function.
>   *nerves cover the human and*
>   *the human*
is a very interesting animal filled with fighting. we have two hands.

>   *delicate hands*
the hand helps us create everything. if we do not have the hand
we cannot throw the rock, we cannot save the water, cannot hand
something to other humans to eat.

>   *the hand makes us more*
generous and also dangerous.
>   *you cannot throw far. you want to throw farther.*
if you do not have those thoughts, you cannot invent those things.

the throwing concept creates the bow and arrow, the gun, the rocket,
the intercontinental missile
>   *only the human hand can throw.*

>   *the throwing concept is neither good nor bad.*
if you throw a rock at a human you hit them, if you throw clothes and money
>   *the first action of throwing is releasing. you release*
open your hand to throw.

>   *

                              I used my hand to draw a horse
and you said it was not a horse.   it is true
we are most often nervous when faced with a hand.

we scald and grip.   hit the tennis ball again and again.

                      horses have four hooves and no hands.

I drew hands onto the horse and I learned
                      gunpowder comes from the disappointment
of having hands.

you told me a horse cannot throw a tennis ball over a chain-link fence

                      and the horses laugh. look at us throwing
ourselves into space.   this is a good lie

we tell ourselves but what if

you hit them.
                  hit with your palm first, an open strike.

*

the human is the hand function. I used my hand to draw a horse
and you said it was not a horse. *nerves cover the human and* it is true
we are most often nervous when faced with a hand. *the human
is a very interesting animal filled with fighting. we have two hands.*

we scald and grip. *delicate hands* hit the tennis ball again and again.
*the hand helps us create everything. if we do not have the hand
we cannot throw the rock, we cannot save the water, cannot hand
something to other humans to eat.* horses have four hooves and no hands.

I drew hands onto the horse and I learned *the hand makes us more
generous and also dangerous.* gunpowder comes from the disappointment
of having hands. *you cannot throw far. you want to throw farther.
if you do not have those thoughts, you cannot invent those things.*

you told me a horse cannot throw a tennis ball over a chain link fence.
*the throwing concept creates the bow and arrow, the gun, the rocket,
the intercontinental missile* and the horses laugh. look at us throwing
ourselves into space. *only the human hand can throw.* this is a good lie

we tell ourselves but what if *the throwing concept is neither good nor bad.
if you throw a rock at a human you hit them, if you throw clothes and money*
you hit them. *the first action of throwing is releasing. you release
open your hand to throw.* hit with your palm first, an open strike.

Paige Quiñones
Aubade

Longing is an improper bit in the mouth.
You didn't know the word in English,
so I explain: *for horses, it's nothing like when I put*

my fingers in and grab your jaw and pull.
They've got this perfect empty space.

When you stand, naked, to grab a book or
a cigarette, I remind myself to memorize
your particular tilt. *No man knows his end,*

my father often says to me. It's about dying,
but I hear: a lover can exit a doorway, a lover

can unwittingly click his teeth
against yours, the first filly to win the Derby
can be named Regret—mine is in the form

of hard muscle and foam.

Troy Varvel
Complete

How about a space-a a
      vac   vv
          Vacuum?

a
      vacancy f
for me to
t
         Try something?
Talk. To as
to ask you wh
to ask a question about
why ew
why you, during those school years,
browbe
      browbeat me in the schoolyard,
your knuckles churning
my cheekbones into a purple-blue egg.

Le
let me answ
let me tell you
      words now spear
      into my tongue. Un
unable to shoot strai
shoot straight out.

Let me ans,
gi
                        give me time
li
looking at m
looking at me you wouldn't kn
know this about me. Th
That I sti
still clutch those days
in my fist.   Ju
                        Just like you dinn
                        didn't always sh sh
                        show
how you sin
            Sing?
how you would single me out,
silence me in dirt and chain link.
I   I
        I know I soak up
a lot of patience—I
                        I'm not what you thaw
what you thought of whe
thought of when you said
you wanted a friend who ma
made you hang onto every word.
If you g
If yo
I
        if you g
                Go?
if you give me a few more
seconds than others, I co
                What?

Please I
Please I know what I wan
what I want to say. I kno
I know you don't fe
don't feel the sa
feel the s

torrin a. greathouse

Abecedarian Requiring Further Examination Before a Diagnosis Can Be Determined

—*after Natalie Diaz*

Antonym for me a medical
book. Replace all the punctuation—
commas, periods, semicolons—with question marks.
Diagnosis is just apotheosis with sharper
edges. New name for a myth already lived in.
For the sake of *thoroughness*, I have
given until my veins cratered. Tests administered for:
HIV, cirrhosis, glucose, cancer, creatine, albumin, iron, platelets.
I've slept for days, wired to machines. Had my piss filtered for stray proteins
just to be safe. Still, inside my body—
kingdom with poisoned wells. I want anything but an elegy
lining my bones. I just want to be a question this body can answer.
My new doctor writes one referral, then another, still
no guesses. A man in a scowl & lab coat
offers yoga, more painkillers. Suggests
PTSD could be the cause—of chronic pain, my limp, of migraines,
quickened pulse & blood-glittered coughs, of seizures
rattling me inside my skin—O,
syndrome of my perfect & unbroken
transgender arm. They checked my hormones too. Yes.
Unfathomable—a suffering I did not choose. Must be gender, this
vacancy my body makes of its own flesh. How I vanish from myself.
We search for a beginning to this story & find only a history of breakage
x-rays cannot explain. Some girls are not made, but spring from the dirt:
yearling tree already scarred from its branch's severance.
Zygote of red clay that rain washes into a river of blood.

Michael M. Weinstein
Anniversary

Do June again, for you have not gotten it quite.

                    What a passionless substance

       this absence is, colors

               summer in as if by number:

lemonade, trampledgrass, smalt—which is a deep & nearly

unforgivable blue. As it latens it dawdles, collects

          all what's abandoned, the sunlight does.

       An o'clock / an ochre filter.

               The fossilized playground structures'

rusty spines. What extinct species of verb were once

             mine? Run, jump, climb. Up the hot

metal bend of the slide. Shiny violence, this wistfulness—wants to put flesh on

the bones of it: feathers, scales, fingernails.

            To see in the ginkgo tree's stinking seeds what

the world was. A substance, yet passionless. Not wanting anything but to be truly without us,

for a branch tip to shoot out a leaf—

thus may each pollen cone release

its impeccable sporophylls, as it has always done—and go on

doing & doing that. June

was all strung up, like the ghostly diaphanous

slips on the fire escape at dusk—the undershirt barely

swaying like a rabbi praying

in his sleep, so sheer you saw the moon

sweat through, the dark all round—on our hopes for it.

A maculate

summer night far from the center, real far, almost close to the airport,

sprawl of vacant lots & used car dealerships is what we got.

An o'clock

like the other o'clocks. Except we had thought

I could walk. Pale prince in a kingdom of silverware I became

that night, that summer,

sat up

coloring the window: dark & dark & dark,

a deep substance, passionless. Swallowing

none of the vast sweep of feeling feasting on the joists of my

half-life, June just went on

polishing the horizon like a knife—a lost continent's edge,

Ability—agleam & neatly

placed back into the velvet drawer of night.

& maybe the trees, too—so black we

can't see them now—believed

they'd been promised a different arrangement,

not to kneel still as penitents until

the sky lucidly, scrupulously drops

its breathless dioxides. We had dreamed July

temperate: all ice cream & iridescence, even mosquitoes'

tinselflickering wings at our elbows expected, somehow correct. But the fact

a plastic sac

of powdered-freezedried-then-diluted monoclonal antibodies stolen

from a mouse now drips

down into the roots of me—

that this substance, passionless, attacks

every cell

with its runoff of chemical snow—

feels like an outside joke. A laughter / a slaughter.

Like how I was somebody's daughter. How once we watched each other

put on a dress

with a terrible earnestness

& nothing anywhere breathing.

I was a mummy back then: someone

had painted a code on my body, a face on my face,

someone crushed spices into my absences, someone rinsed my insides with palm wine,

& I lay waiting

to disappear, or change.

You took the name

I gave you, and the thought that you carry it

over the fields of your whole time

on earth cuts into me

like that post-IV ache in the vein, won't go away.

How to come back from that.

How to go out, like folks do, for a walk

—lemonade, trampledgrass—& not feel gone from it, not

take the whole gorgeous aftermath

personally? I try

to do June again, only this time we're not underwater—

down deep in the cold seeps, the abyssal

plain with its hagfish & boneworms & hundreds of atmospheres pressed on our hearts.

Remember?

How fear was our warmth down there, our shared

nourishment detritus of the secret

drifting relentlessly into our mouths, unspeakable.

Now it is out,

hung on these beached ribs, extinct & free,

I carry the ocean inside. In that vascular dark,

so much of my flesh was imaginary.

No one could see me. Only you could see me.

Isabel Ries Neal
All Winter

All winter I pined.
I coned, caved.

I held my bridle lip,
my bride. My mouth,

my bride. Rough
jeans. Jeer.

Rubbed
with bristle brush.

Fed feed.

What if, fearing being led,
I lead?

Johann Sarna
Love

You have plans to drive
to the part of the city you've
never seen for a gorgeous
donut. This is how it is
reinforced. The helicopters
suspended over the freeway
the people solidifying
in light. Some of them have made
children who work
in the prairie provinces
where the cows freeze to death.
Some wait like
repossessed toucans in a
stained hangar, trembling
in the hollow space.
Nights offer this stance.
In this way I have learned
when tank honks on the corner
I will strive for tank commander, that
I am this terrible truism
of striving. So when you lay yourself
down like a rail I will also have
the right to say the wind
rides me. But you can change
the world's impress on you
by hoisting something heavy.
Often I look forward to the
final set of deadlifts. I am

a mallet, a trowel in the
day's calloused hand. Don't
question smoothing these
minutes over. Dandelions are
missing. Amber
alert in my belly.
Mild terrain to the west
I might devour. We make space
for the light to know us.
From the darkness
I can sense the reparations
we are prepared to make to the year
and you said there's so much
we might learn from the octopus
after he has tussled on the pale
seabed, tiptoeing back to his
hole like a silent actor. Yet I lock
myself with the berry, with the flame
in the unfinished foundation. Pits
everywhere support pillars of sky
while today marks the start of
being the most beautiful
marauder. There's a moon. Tsars
in the books, friends who calibrate
the F-35s especially. It's enough to say
fuck this brunch, this croissant's
view of the hills. I don't mind.
I keep a river on me, I load
my mouth with Cellini's
imperious salamander. And one
revels in this happy
sitting, and you sleeping
in the next room, I'll need

a new notebook soon
for this indulgent feeling
away from the blinking tower, the satellite
in the time of year one feels
attacked by the mystery
of pollen, necessary before indulgence.
Indulging in what? You sleep,
a monogrammed toothpick on
the rim of a volcano. I trot,
a bawling hedgehog
nosing for cover. It's a phase,
we learn invincibility is amoral
there really is a payout
if you hammer your nose hard enough
if you sell the great accident
of the yacht fire to the proper authorities.
Eventually we might all boast: my son! who is
standing in the face of the sky! and
mean ourselves, terrified by the shine, the star's
mind roiling in the creek. Wake up
my love. No gurneys or blackout
festival goers today. There's no train
here but we have these souls called
neighbors floating tentatively over the
courtyard and our mouths
empty of despair. Think: you,
the one receiving transmission
not above anything
but distanced from the gerbils
and grass snakes. Come
home with the groceries
and together we will stumble through
the transformation of these tomatoes.

Who can duck my cant? You agree
Monday night is a most sinister
clearing in the week's forest. The baby
piranha takes out the massive
loan called aquarium. You were happy
to be the benevolent lender
and do not wish violence on
anything but it can't be helped, this
scuttling back and forth over
the teal patterns of paisley over
the rain heavy earth. Not even
called rain at that point
when we've locked ourselves into bed with
the minor noises of peace time.
So later we walk, sound, miles of
shits left to take, over the grates
and stripes. A red bean cake hot
on a hot June day. A naked biker at noon.
Who were you anyway, to lick me so
familiarly? Tankers, marzipan, denuded
and ineffective facemasks. Talking
sun into each other. It was prescient
caterwauling. It was disregarding
our chambers. I was something living
for the next bite. You were bowing
gently to the roots. With a hand out to day.
Making some bargain with the sky, an
exchange past me and my vocabulary
broken by that banter.

Erin Marie Lynch
St. Helens

Did what I was told; polished silverware

with blue paste; saw myself in the mirror

and turned away, thinking, *seeing herself*

naked, she turned away; soaked my blood-

stained underwear in the sink; sat quiet at

church like moss on the car hood; opened

the shoebox that held my great-grandma's

long dark braid, severed a century ago by

a kitchen knife; waded the creek bed down

to where it fled beneath the highway; read

about the Vanishing Hitchhiker, a girl who

sits in the back seat and whispers, *St. Helens*

will erupt in May; let all the shadows deep

in my closet press closely, hissing, *show us*

your ugly heart, lift up your shirt; wondered

whether ghosts chose to be; lay on my back

by the maple tree; felt the neighbor's shape

fall across me as he said, *nothing like a pretty*

girl reading; was allowed by distance to hide

the volcano, small and cold, with my hand.

Jessica Yuan
Disorientation

If I make it this far.
If I make it home to the sublet
with Styrofoam paneling the shower
and five women hiding the hotplate.
If I make it past the crowds
most like me, drinking away
their weekday nights on the strength
of the dollar. If I make it through,
dodging the long shadows of men
before they touch my shadow.
Thick asphalt grains biting into brick
on a hillside I cannot name.
Sidewalk patched and flattened
by whoever owns the nearest edge.
After the tight history of the center
are the peripheries exposed,
streetlights hard on the avenue
wrapping the slope then piercing
straight through the roofline;

he saw me eating a peach
at the base of a monument
covering its history for the night.
He offered to drive me home
then he drove over a river
I had not crossed, while the city
spun out from the tight nest
of the center, after the alleys

straighten into boulevards
and windows bloom full-faced.
He drove down to the fourth
sub-basement garage and stood me up
on the tenth story, my highest point
that summer, everywhere I crawled
at ground level fading below
out of light. His window
had everything but the way back.
So I did. So I did it. I had no map
and he took my map.
He handed me his business card
and he drove me home after;

until I emerge from the bridge
marked by a tulip where the stairs
stiffen into ladders below the moon.
I passed the archive and its courtyard
vaulted over with yellowing glass.
I crossed the valley paved
from brick to granite, the season
from cherries to peach. I passed
the courtyard for peacocks
and courtyard for chickens.
I passed the wide smooth scar
of concrete over the tunnel beneath.
I wore my face like a printed shroud
scrimmed over the scaffolding
of a monument's renovation.
When the monument emerges,
who keeps the shroud? My shroud
is tired and has become the real thing.
I keep it trailing behind me.

Sophia Stid
Apophatic Ghazal

I have written this poem and made it sound worse than it was. Then better.
I have put in a gun. I have written it out again. I have made myself say *no*

when I didn't. I have tried to write why I didn't say *no* when I could have.
I have tried to explain the back of my neck, that feeling, when you know

something bad is about to happen, that animal revolt. Once, I felt a rattlesnake.
I mean I felt before I saw. I mean my body told me. But back to that night. No

other way it could have gone, or so it seems now. It seemed different then.
The restaurant, white tablecloth, rack of lamb, quiet loud as velvet, no

prices on the menu. His house just down the street. I went there with him.
Which is what I'm supposed to say now, the thing I did that I should not

have done. Only when he closed the door behind us, my body spoke.
Reminding me of—what? The back of my neck. *Not*

here, I told my body, meaning, *wait till I'm alone to talk like that.*
And it listened. Years of attrition trained my body to wait, to stop, no

argument. I stayed in my chair. I never said the secret. His tongue was a fish.
His tongue was a fish in my mouth, heavy wet muscle. I said nothing

when he splashed whiskey into the crystal glass. *That's my father,* he said.
Pointing. On the wall, old gold frames, photographs, the flag, I said nothing

although I knew the face from the newspaper I said nothing. I thought.
The door (oak) locked. The walls (stone) thick. My throat was taught not

to shout in a quiet place, and when it was time, I found it could not.
Would not. Later, I had to forgive my throat. What you think happened did not

happen. Instead, a sound, a shot, a car backfiring.
He looked up. I fought to my feet, the floor, the door. I never said no

but my whole body meant it. He could hear the sound outside but not
my body. Never said no. There is the law. And then there is something better.

Imani Davis
Everything Must Go

—after Xandria Phillips

as is tradition for the women / of my blood, / I shop too much. will
sacrifice / a paycheck like a lamb for the chance to conjure up / a fresh
silhouette. & I am supposed to hate / this about us. the nerve: to wrap our
bodies in myths / we can't afford. but I want to / make peace with this. I
want to make peace with my grandmother's gentle back / -room dedicated
solely to the choir / of her hatboxes, quiet revelations / lining each wall. all
day, she darts between the news & the home shopping network, unsure
/ whether to spend her pension or her prayer. once, she fled / a country
ribboned by war / as if it were a dressing room. practiced walking in
america / -n shoes until balance became her. to this day, she nests / for her
daughters until there is nothing left / on the racks. stores enough patent-
leather & lace to clothe every ghost / she left in Honduras. & who could
call such a selfless love / a waste? still, my mother say grandma got too
much / space in her heart. too many shelves inside of her she can't wait to
fill. / we have this in common. on weeknights, I midnight / scroll across
landscapes of pixelated fabric / without direction. check for sales like my
life / depends on it. desire a beauty / aimless as light. each morning, I wake
wanting / to script a new creation story / across my skin. dare the day to
reinvent itself until / everything that's hurt me is a stain / washed clean.
sometimes, the mirror is the only place / I decide what happens / to my
body. here, I sketch myself into a velvet miracle / no one dare touch. the
night / the thief undresses me, every drawer in my chest lay empty / as a
scream. how to replace what is stolen / when it is the body / itself? officer
asks what / I wore that night & i think of my grandma's urgent gaze / in
macy's. here is its root: we shop to find the look that might finally keep
us / safe. if there is always a danger to outrun, praise the choice / of heels
for the chase. praise the good shoe & the stature / it lends me tonight.
praise the pomp & circumstance of ripping the tag off / a brand-new skin.

my grandmother & I dressed ourselves out / of deaths already tailored to fit. if this is a sin, / I'll take one in every color. so bless every tattered thread / of this love. bless the thousand shopping carts I've filled & emptied / communion of fabric gathered / at my feet. after we leave the mall, grandma asks me to say grace over dinner. I take bread, / & break it. say: / this is my body, taken back. I do this in remembrance / of me.

Aldo Amparán
Thanatophobia, or Sleep Addresses His Brother

> *No duerme nadie por el mundo.*
> —Federico García Lorca

Night: the world boils. Men
    toss sleepless
        in their sheets like stars.

        Because I look down
    where a man holds his only son
among the spillage

of buildings, & children
    sitting on debris
        after the bombs

        cast their shadows
    onto stone, & the boy hangs
from his father's arms, his father's hand

folded to the open neck, & the open eyes
    like cold nickels look past me, past
        the white sheet of linen.

        How terrible
    the fabric that veils
the end. How terrible

the night for him, the sleepless,
    Brother. When an American soldier
        swallows a grenade which bursts

as it slips down his throat, a Mexican
immigrant, a woman beaten
half to death for stealing

a pomegranate, breaks
the fruit's skin open, red
from her wounds

like the inside of the fruit,
or the inside of the soldier,
& doctors put to sleep

a girl to replace her heart with a new
beating. Soon that artificial
sleep turns the same terrible

fabric. Her mother, quiet
as a desert in the hall,
admires Wojnarowicz's *Untitled*

(Buffalo), that great beast at the edge
of the photograph suspended
in air forever.

& the girl's father reaches
her mother's arm to keep her
from plunging off the rooftop

to fall into you,
Brother. I know nothing
but impermanent rest.

How do you do it
each time you take & take & wrap
your permanence around

sleep? Brother,
you terrify me.
You make my heart

gallop like buffaloes
in the white desert, their large bodies
advancing their fall.

Simon Shieh
Kindness Comes Too Easily to Wicked Men

In every ballroom, he is the chandelier. No,

he is the song
that everyone only knows the chorus of.

Beautiful,
relentless.

He dresses as a dead soldier
every Halloween.
In the army, he says

*you are dirt under the nails
of your country.*

My mother wants him dead.
The family of a young
girl wants him dead.

In the pockets
of his old fatigues, a torn zodiac

and a rusted
metal spoon. Never

in my life did I believe
I knew him.
Once

in a fit of rage,
he named every star in the sky
after a dead man. Premature

blessing.
One night, in a Taiwan hospital

a man

cut my mother open and took
my body out.
Deliverance.

Years later, she will tell me
we never remember the men
who we cannot forget.

He gave me a necklace
of teeth. He laughs

each time someone says
the word *God.*
Every day

I guess his favorite color
and every day
I get it wrong.

Mercy sweet throat.
Mercy blackbird.

He once wrote a song about me
        in the middle of the night.

            When I sing it, a black snake slithers
      from my mouth.

Jackson Holbert

Letter Sent to a Friend Who Frequently Requires Horses but Has None

Although I cannot
remember you coming
through the wheat thick
as the space between
tomato and daughter I can
say that even under
the worst reigns
I would have lent you horses.
And after a terrible day
I would have led
half of them down
to the lake with you
to drink the awful water
that tastes like pencils.

Thomas McGuire

Four Ways of Looking at Magpie—A Most Becoming Bird

> *You did not kill the fish only to keep alive and to sell for food, he thought.*
> *You killed for pride and because you are a fisherman. You loved him when*
> *he was alive and you loved him after. If you love him, it is not a sin to kill*
> *him. Or is it more?*
> —Ernest Hemingway, *The Old Man and the Sea*

1.

Dried all our wet articles this fine Day, / Capt Lewis out with a View to see
the Countrey / and its productions, gone all day; / killed a Buffalow and
a remarkable Bird / of the *Corvus* Species, Magpy. / a butifull thing, this
magpy.   —after Wm. Clark's entry dated 17 Sept, 1804

2.

one of the hunters killed a bird
of the *Corvus* genus and order of the pica
about the size of a jack-daw   with a tale remarkably long,
                    beautifully variegated.
these birds seldom appear in parties of more than three or four;
     most usually at this season, they range single as the halks (ravens)
          and other birds of prey commonly do—
from its sleak appearance I believe too
                    its usual food is flesh—

Pica hudsonia has an agreeable note
     something like a gold-winged blackbird,
          a note not disagreeable, though loud—
               twait twait twait, twait; twait, twait twait, twait.

Flying, this bird does not spread its tail
    & aloft its wing motions recall the Jay-bird's—
(its flying note—*tah, tah, tah, tah tah, tah, tah, tah*)
and the wings have nineteen feathers,
    forming a darkly colored triangle when spread—
dark but not jet or shining black; darker yet is the wing's underside.
The upperside of the wing is a dark blackish or bluish green
        sometimes tinting soft bluish or light orange yellow
    in different light exposures—a kalediscope of color.

The plumage of the tale figures twelve feathers of equal lengths by pairs;
here, too, the feather bottom changes, refracting different portions of light:
    towards their extremity, these feathers hue orange green,
        then shaded, pass to a reddish indigo blue,
    and at their extremity assume the green of mutability—
the tinges of these beautiful feathers are not unlike
    but equally rich as the peacock's tints of blue and green—
        Magpie is a most becoming bird.

        —after Meriwether Lewis's entry dated 17 Sept, 1804

3.

Meriwether's measure of a magpie:

	Ft	In
from tip to tip of wing	1	10
Do. beak to extremity of tale	1	8 ½
of which the tale occupys		11
from extremity of middle toe to hip		5 ½

4.

Ordway's journal, Wednesday, 3rd April 1805 (clear and pleasant)

The articles which was to be Sent back
to the States in the Big Barge was packed
and boxed up ready to go on board.

To which entry, the Magpie requests a favor of reply:
Of the live animals caged & shipped,
only the prairie dog and one of the four magpies
reached Mr. Jefferson alive—
an ill omen forsooth.

In turn President Jefferson sent Charles Wilson Peale the marmot
& the surviving magpie for his museum of curiosities in Philadelphia.

Sara Elkamel
Field of No Justice

Though they will be reborn
each morning with the sun,

the dead remain obsessed
with the image of a single rose

by a crocodile's open mouth.

A wail from the corner of the room
usurps the room.

Give me a mouth; I want to talk!

said the dead woman to the scale.

The heart on the scale is the heart of a sparrow.
My heart is the heart of a sparrow!
The sparrow was unremarkable; I cannot give you her name.
When I fell, she switched my heart for hers.
Mine was a clay heart the size of the sun.
Ask the sun, just ask the sun!
The sparrow's feather heart is not my heart.
My heart knew nothing for certain.
Loved nothing for certain.
My clay heart did not know its own name.
My clay heart envied goslings their nests.
Envied mothers their sons.

Smothered every fire before its hour.
My clay heart cursed the heart of my mother.
I stayed a child to have a child.
I kept everything secret.
My clay heart licked the milk off the mouths of little children.
I chewed the hair off my knuckles to make the hands usable.
I tried to be a woman.
My clay heart thawed one night, I saw it.
I gave a boat to a boatless man, and at the lips of water took it back.
I wrapped the heart of my love in white muslin cloth and buried it with the others.
I made a remedy for remembering and drank one half in the morning and one half at night.
I couldn't move.
I gave myself running feet. Even remember how I did it. I scraped sand off my
toes and mixed it with pulverized red pepper. I spooned it into the river even
though they said this causes a person to run from place to place, until she runs
herself to death.
I couldn't move.
The prayers I whispered into the walls bounced back.
I am not pure, I am not pure, I am not pure, I am not pure.

They weighed the wrong heart and found it
lighter than a feather.

To the field of reeds! said gently
the forty-two gods of the feather.

There was water behind the door.

But my heart,
I said—

Find the sparrow, said Osiris
stroking softly the crocodile.

The sparrow soared freely
above the cliffs

and the light fell on all of us.

Michaela Coplen
Gate Control

The gruesome death I mind the least is being buried alive.
When the god of the underworld steals a girl, he takes her by the waist.
The month I bled, I bound my mid as if to hold it in.
Born too soon & out of breath & so in want of swaddle.
I want it now & constant. I want tourniquet-tight.
When I first fucked an older man, he made me stop performing.
He pressed one hand down on my chest, the other one inside
& crooned *good girl* into my warmth as one might soothe a foal.
Adam. I'm sorry it didn't work & never made me love you.
Leaving is nothing like jet plane; it's more a heavy chopper.
I maintain that there is too much sky. I can't be unconvinced.
& Still I have that splinting urge, to hold the hurting thing.
Pain & any other feel are numbed by enough compression.
I imagine release as a greyhound derby—all the gates are flung

Catherine Pond
Forest Horse

He was gone by then, gone with girlhood,
like an apparition, until one night
outside Woodstock, I heard shuffling in the branches
outside the kitchen window
and saw the glowing body, silver with time,
emerge from behind a lone pine.
I walked out the back door. Cold
air lifted my hair. We were so close
we almost touched. I was waiting for him to remember
who I was, to remember why he resented me.
Instead there was fear in his eyes. I could tell he had been out there
a long time. He moved closer, his breath turning to steam.
I reached out and touched his cheek.
Like a child he heaved against me, and I held him.
In the silence there was a sick sister,
a collapsed house. I couldn't.
I thought about the long years between our last visit.
I wanted to explain how lonely I had been,
how loneliness had made me
mean, unreliable. Had driven me deeper in.
Even now, being with him
meant abandoning my family,
who were gathering inside the house,
waiting to serve dinner,
wondering where I was. I knew
he might never appear again,
or only after a long snow, in the middle of the night—

and that I would love him forever,
not in spite of the way he stayed gone
for so long, but because of it.

Liza Flum
Nuptial Dive

A man and a woman jump from a plane

on TV together, strapped to instructors

like babies on parents' chests: they fall

face-first through blue atmosphere, cameras

catching their screams, then fields:

in the landing zone the man tries standing,

tumbles on his back: then they kiss in the grass

under lenses: these two in their dropped

nest of parachutes, entwined arms: "Love

comes from falling," say love's manufacturers:

but the hummingbird's nuptial dive

is obsessive. He flies over the female, again,

again, grazing her head, then he zooms, climbs

seventy feet, plummets to hover above her crown.

In the book on my lap this flight is hand-drawn:

X marks the female, treasure and cipher. I study

the flightpath. In the picture it looks like a fishhook,

and he rises as if he were a fish, caught, reeled in.

Does it burn him, too, this dizzying world? What

compels him? The bird flies up, yes,

but is it also love that yanks him? Or need? Is X

glad to see him? Is she afraid?

When I chose to marry you it felt like a jump

into nothing. It was not to impress you. It was hardly choosing.

Like standing on the high dive. To return to our life

happening below I had to jump. I only remember

how poorly I did it. The rough board under my toes

as I stepped forward. How I fell alone.

How the water lifted around me on impact like a veil.

*

I never told you my grandmother

        was a trick diver. Her act: Disappearing

                Mermaids. The secret: to stay submerged

    in an airtight chamber, counting to one hundred, then rise

with a smile, arms spread,

            amid ripples. Applause. Over and over.

      I found the room underwater—meet me there.

—Nominated by the University of Utah
Creative Writing Program

Rachel Busnardo
I Came from beneath the Sea

This isn't my last time
as the seabather's eruption,

my slow rash tramping
forward in kaiju custom.

I came vibrating, as a fly
threatens to spoil the cake.

Do Not Enter scribbled
on my body like a receipt

printed on dappled bone.
Can you hear me? I came

with sirens, octaves
of intensity, wild chants

in the face of effortless
power tonguing their cud.

White pepper dribble
on their chin; bits of yellow

wallpaper souring their lips.
How did we become so unraveled?

Pentagram carved on my chest
like a brooch; me,

the ilk of the damned,
you, the pitchfork as Earth

sprouts another fire, another
hurricane, another man

just doing his best. I came
from the hues of strata

holding carbon like an omen.
Blood cries from the holy mother

deafened by the yawps of wolves;
my own teeth gapped and yellow,

will you put me down too?
The largest crater on the moon

is on its darkside, an eye facing
away, will you too roll

your eyes back into your own
universe? I came from plastic:

broken syringes, broken
pots and wax foliage, broken

toys carving up the beach.
I came from constructs:

gold dusted pizza, money,
and borders. I came with

purpose, smelters, and roots
protruding from my body.

I came for chaos—
my hatred prayer;

I come to your shores:
a single scale in the sand—

see how it catches the light.

Jesús I. Valles
Gatorade, pepino y limon

your scent makes my mouth crave itself becoming the bank where you run before you empty
worse, it makes me write about you or myself as a river, which I only know platonically
as a way out of a country, so now I'm a Mexican writing about becoming a river

or being a river, or wanting water from you, or wanting you to drain into me
explicitly, to have you cum in my mouth, specifically, to lose my head to you
make your thighs a guillotine for me until I can't remember any smell that isn't you ending

god, I am thirsting—I was saying I was a river, or the bank of one, and I love the word tributa
I put two Gatorades outside your door, pepino y limon, because you were sick, a tribute
to summers you've likely spent like me, chubby and boy and Tajin'd, remember?

anyway, how could I not crave something like you, hungry for your mama's boy sweet smile,
your eyes always some cute distant, and fuck! the uniform; basketball shorts and white t-shirt
last night and how could I resist running to you if you smell like every place my world began?

Zach Linge
Fingers on a Gay Man

A pair of adolescent boys grabs a rabbit to shear off its ears. It doesn't matter why, whether they're sad or from the city. What matters is what they do with their hands: hold the blade, hang the rabbit by its ears. But the rabbit says, "I met a truck-stop priest in Mississippi outside Books-A-Million, should I tell you what he said?" And the boys pause to consider, so he continues, "We sat into the night talking about anything: his gay ex-wife who practices witchcraft, masturbation with vacuum hoses, his fetish for boys' leg hairs—like your own!" They giggle at this and scream, set the rabbit down, and listen. "The priest in his collar and cross necklace spoke, though his face transformed: he grew freckles where there weren't any freckles; he grew beards where his chin was smooth; and his eyes were more ancient than all the lakes in Mississippi." *What did he say? What did he say?* the boys demand, wanting to learn, more than anything. Continues the rabbit, "The faces spoke, not the priest, in voices that traveled to my brain. They taught me lessons. First, that every soul is a thread in a cloth that floats through black everything, sparkling like snow into a lake. So you, and I, and everyone we know are iterations of these souls, these cloths, some newly woven, and some old." The boys: *What else did the faces say?* The rabbit: "They said that they and I were of a single cloth, of the type who dies and rises again." *And what about us? What about us?* demand the boys, and the rabbit jumps off the rock and runs because the boys hold a knife and can't recognize a parable or my face, however human.

Jae Nichelle
Three Churches Burn in Louisiana

when two or more Black people gathering in the name of
preservation agree, it's a law. I pass two or more Black people
on the street, we form a congregation

built on head nods and anonymity. my congregation not the
forgiving type. an attempt to burn two or more Black people
gathering in the name of preservation

warrants my congregation knocking on your door on a
Sunday morning just to tell you your bloodline ain't shit.
now it's a law. a church is where two or more Black

people gather. a church unseen cannot be burned, it's a law.
my congregation resurrects churches & blackens your eye
faster than you can look at us. look at us.

my congregation don't testify against other members of the
congregation. that's a law. an embrace between two or more
Black people is silent worship of our Black

and our bodies. two or more Black people agree to whoop
the ass of the next person who tries us. I'm tired. I need two
or more Black people to embrace me.

we save each other in this congregation. we don't wait for
external justice. we don't seek restoration. two or more Black
people gathering in the name

of preservation have died for just that. my congregation disguises a laying of hands as a handshake. they're praying for me. me and the still warm ground.

—Nominated by *Washington Square Review*

Andrew Collard
Badlands Flashback

We woke blank as though   we'd been born there,
at the end of praise, no ode
persisting to anything,   among trails of eroded rock,

off-white, that we walked despite the glare
of whatever past refused us,   surrounded by
    a shortgrass thick with rattling. Our every

footstep resounded   like a burst of comm static,
unsettling the heavy air. Beyond us,   the state highway,
        two lanes through desert,

could've been Colorado or Dakota,   the painted booth
            cars queued before
    to buy passes   denoting the entrance

to Four Corners, or Yosemite.   I can't trick myself
        into remembering it any better,
can no longer locate us   by the type of wildlife

dead   on the roadside, or
        the orange barrels lined up like birthday candles
on certain routes.   What I know

            is we left
to look for god   or his replacement, and ended up
impatient for arrival, as if   distance itself

might be disposable,   like some grease-stained wrapper
        that once swaddled fries, as if
we could each, as lovers,   divorce ourselves

from the process of our bodies—
        the old mistake   of presuming movement
had the power to erase   the taste of emptiness

hanging in our mouths like rotten teeth.   What I know
        is I am moving, again,   toward confronting
what my body has become to you,   which parts of me

have become someone else's   as we dissipate
        into our components, the minerals,   or deposits,
whatever it is they say   this flesh and blood is made of.

—Nominated by Western Michigan University

Cameron Quan Louie
Shaving before we go to visit your father

for the last time,
what surprised me
the whole day was only
how little I wanted
to talk about it. Strange
for our kind to come up
blank given the shot
to speak. But as I
replaced the razor
and wiped a little
steam from the mirror,
I thought, oh, this is it.
The largest chamber
of the heart of the weakness
of men. I shelter there
until it's impossible.
I cry into the shoulder
of my mother's summer
blouse. I sit in the driver's
seat of my car after
breakfast. Absurd
to eat breakfast. And
that something as neat
as a line, his patient
colleagues at the clinic,
waiting for a turn
to thank his portrait, forms
on its own. Not long,

they take him off water,
put him on some thickened
crystal jelly. Trouble
swallowing. And to lean
on words like peace or
process. Afterwards.
And that the afterwards
in our backyard spits
yellow blossoms out
of its thick stalks,
catastrophe of promise
that shows no sign
of slowing down.

Daniel Barnum
Would I Change All I Know for Unknowing

east where you're never going back. houses
on the hollow. drinking enough to kill
yourself. teenage bullshit. wanting to kiss
your best friend. twilight of the tire iron.
dad yelling *you're not sick, are you?* deer down
the trailway at season's end-of-slaughter.
in piles. unreal as your fever feels. path off
of that same road, where mom broke her
arm one winter. fell on february
ice. didn't realize for days after—
said that it hardly felt like anything
at first. lamplight from our neighbor's front porch;
windows spectral the woods' leafless maples.
in memory, this all happens more than once.

        in memory, this all happens more than once:
        windows spectral the woods' leafless maples,
     the lamplight fits from our neighbor's front porch.
         they said they hardly heard anything
          through the ice. didn't realize for days after.
           gone one winter, well into february.
       that same road where mom had broken into her
           unreal. pile-up of fever dreams. no path
          out from that season's end. the slaughter
         sound of dad yelling. *I'm not sick deep down*
I think, lit in unironic love for my best friend. he tires
        of me. our teenage bullshit. he wants to kiss
         girls down at the hollow. I'll drink to kill
off east coast as point of no return. that's home.

in memory, this all happens more than once: east, where you're never going back. houses.
windows. spectral, the woods' leafless maples on the hollow. drinking enough to kill
the lamplight fits from our neighbor's front porch. yourself. teenage bullshit. wanting to kiss
(they said they hardly heard anything) your best friend. twilight of the tire iron
through the ice. didn't realize for days after. dad yelling *you're not sick, are you?* deer down.
gone one winter, well into february, the trailway at season's end-of-slaughter.
that same road where mom had broken into pieces. real as your fever feels. path off
of its unreal pile-up of fever dreams. no path. the same road where mom broke her-
self out from that season's end. winter like an army. slaughter. the february
sound of dad yelling, *I'm not sick.* deep down, ice. *didn't realize*—for days after
I think, lit in unironic love for my best friend. he tires. says that it hardly felt like anything
with me. our teenage bullshit. he wanted to kiss first. lamplight from the neighbor's front porch;
girls down at the hollow. I'll drink to kill windows, spectral the woods' leafless maples,
off east coast as point of no return. that's home. in memory, this all happens more than once.

—Nominated by *Muzzle Magazine*

Michael Torres
All-American Mexican

All I wanted was a Cadillac on chrome, real
diamonds in my ears, and someone to call
my name through a crowd. Instead, me
and the homies drove to the mall
in my hatchback, rocking dog tags with
Tupac on 'em; we lived for his
Westside fingers. We stopped at "Nothing

but Silver," a store where I sifted through
glinting trays of jewels for princess-cut
earrings. No one asked if we needed help but
everyone stared a long time. No one called
our names so we took new ones. Swallowed
them whole and they grew inside us. Inside
the food court bathroom our new names
bloomed black from Magnum markers;
inside stalls I practiced the *R* the *E* the *M* the
E the *K*. Our names too real for us to contain.
We left and I was glad my hatchback's
bubbled-up window tint distorted our faces.
Everything is always up for interpretation.
Yesterday I ran

an image search of the white boy from tenth
grade who said I looked like a dog. I wanted
to find him posing in a too-wide tie for a job
his face would tell me he hated.

When I found nothing, I thought he might be
dead, so I looked for a park to sit with my
guilt, wondering if I could've saved him,
had we become friends instead, had I helped

retrieve his stack of notes blown apart
by the wind. I am mostly filled with fantasies
where I'm the hero: a parade and a Coup de
Ville to wave from; the Key to the City
the mayor presents on a red velvet pillow.

Now, when I visit home I want to cry but
the homies would notice. And it's not that
they'd laugh and call me a little bitch. No. We
are only as young and thuggish as America
needs us to be. The problem is my homies
wouldn't recognize the puzzle my body has
made of itself.

Let me say it like this: I'm a stuffy June room,
and the homie has only been taught to pry
open whatever might test him. That's real.

Once, I was so real I became a cathedral
at noon. Not the bell itself but the rope pulling
sound from absence. I was only my heart

glowing against the bones holding me back.
Everyone stood to watch. Someone yelled
Fight. Someone said I was scared. But I was

so real I burst into the wind like Fuck
the world. Nothing dissolves like I do.
I came here to create a diversion, to splinter

furniture for the fire. If I'm going to be real,
I am who I've always been: a boy seeking
an orbit to align with. One day I'ma get

POET tatted on my chest. Only instead
of the O, I want a window through which you
can see my childhood backyard, way before
I became something like a souvenir. I might
make my artist ink the tire swing. He says
the worst it'll hurt depends on where
I want to plant the trees.

Caroline Parkman Barr
For Some Time After

The carpet burns against my back

the lightbulbs cool to the touch

and there's something about ceiling fans
I can't quit—dust like cigarette

—the going-around
sounds like my name

chopped in your mouth
when you split my legs

on the floor beside the radiator

—I still see blades spinning
lavender behind closed eyes

phantom crawl of an emery board
breath on my neck

reaching for a glass already
emptied

the image of you
standing in the doorway

boxers to your knees

Kelly McQuain
The Moon in Drag

Moon of hunger, moon of hope, moon of cold nights
and telescopes. Hunter's moon, low-slung and blood-
orange, moon of fruit and moon of thorn. Mother moon
charming a fussy child, werewolf moon fighting
an urge to go wild. Pale thumbprint sugaring
the afternoon's solid blue, neon moon electrifying
all the night through. Full bellied moon, pregnant
with luck or disaster, moon of witch-chant, halo, antler.
Watercolor moon, soft brushstrokes, wet on wet indigo.
Moon inside me, shifting tides. Moon with thumb out
hitching rides. Witch moon bright behind a claw
of dark branches, skinny-dipping moon, back seats,
taking chances. Up-all-night moon, drinker's moon,
moon of worry and moon of deathbed. Holy moon,
traveler's moon, money tucked in a sock, a comb
in its pocket. Moon we aim for with our rockets.
Crossroads moon where the devil plays his tricks,
junky moon, a sweet stargazer fix. Bake-my-misery-
in-butter-and-brown-sugar moon. Juggler's moon,
bills piled high. Evergreen moon, moon that pines
as cool as creek water, moon of second chances,
moon pressing against the night like a drunken lover,
moon that dances. Moon so blue it is the velvet voice
of a lovelorn swain. Moon so cruel you hope to hide
when it shines this way again. Horse thief moon. Moon
that knows the wind's cold rustle by heart, pained moon,
angry moon, quick and sharp. Moon in feather boas and
come-fuck-me pumps, cinched moon, corseted moon,

moon trussed up to the nines, I'll-have-my-way-with-you
moon that laughs as the willows weep, cricket moon,
lake bottom moon, moon that spoons you as you sleep.

Carling McManus
To Eat an Ortolan

For centuries, we've caught the songbirds
in nets and slit their eyes. Darkness
drives them to gorge on grain, their bodies
bloat with fat, soft as fallen figs, no larger
than a curled thumb in a cupped palm.
Then drowned in brandy and plucked,
pan-seared and plated, the bird is eaten
in a single bite, pinched at the beak
and placed, feet first, into the mouth.

It was a priest in the seventeenth century
who first shrouded himself before consuming
an ortolan. He had heard of the fatty meal,
imagined the salt crisped skin on his tongue,
wished for the deep crush of bone
between his teeth. Seated at the table,
the golden body before him, he unfolded
his cloth napkin, draped it over his head
and took the bird into his mouth.

The human body anticipates pleasure
and prepares. As fat cooks and clouds
the air, saliva seeps up from under the tongue,
the pulse of blood flushes the cheeks.
We lick our lips, our eyes black as seeds,
our teeth wait, sharp in our mouths.
Is pleasure greater when braided with shame?
To eat is to sustain, but to feast is to succumb
to another kind of hunger.

In school I skipped class with another girl
to walk the wooded trail and sit where
a tabletop rock overlooked the town.
Barely touching, we watched the birds hang
above us, weightless between branches.
When it began to rain, she held her coat
over our heads. Dry in the darkness, breathing
in the other's breath, we pressed our lips
together, her tongue alive in my mouth.

Andrew David King
Untitled [Iowa field, three crosses]

1.

Iowa field, three crosses: you almost can't see them
against the snow.

I told myself I'd speak freely here.

In this poem, I'd speak freely.

2.

No—it was summer. I'd gone out
to an industrial lot to see if I could find
a giant wire spool
to flip on its side, use as a table in the yard. No luck:

but on a longer way home, three crosses.
A bird for each. My phone
made a little animation afterwards out of the pictures

I took: birds, no birds.

3.

There is no special meaning
in any of this, I tell myself, and you, now.
No meaning
to the iridescent ribbons knotted

to stakes, to the letterforms
in the wood, to the night when four teenagers

broadsided a pickup with the right of way.
None of it.

Nothing special—I heard it first
in a Zen parable, then in the snowplow burying cars
against the curb; late, as usual.

4.

Speaking freely, I wouldn't have had the guts.

I'd dreamed of driving
to the love-handle hills south of Solon, getting out of my car,
taking off my clothes, lying on my back
in the snow. At first

it would hurt (no meaning, nothing
special); I'd regret what I'd know
I couldn't stop doing; then I'd take the regret off, like an undershirt, set it aside.

Someone's headlights would sweep by.
Finger in the back of an old drawer.

5.

True, also,

that I've survived nothing. True as the splatter of red
and green on the floor of the city gym
on disco skate night.

Long before the event ends,
the employees take down the copier-paper signs
with MLK quotations they'd taped to the walls, for MLK Day.
Had anyone seen them

and would they be recycled? Speaking freely, now, is anyone

listening; am I? And if I said something about a fire,
the one hypothermics feel at the end, which it would be wrong
to call a delusion—?

6.

The freezing rain dressed each branch
in a sleeve of ice; each branch had its own
coffin of the sort the rich of one century
favored, if they were of a certain disposition:
coffins with glass windows, so the living
could see the rouged moons of the cheeks,
so the dead could see the signal fires Christ
or Christ's army would set to let them know
it was time to get up. Now, when a car, sloshing
through winter muck and over the slight crest
of the street, shone its light through the trees,
that light was made to violate the usual laws, not
bouncing and diffracting freely off the
wounded, matte surface of living wood in
April, in May, in September, but perambulating
in a pilgrim's circuit each twig's perimeter,
tracing with knifelike steadiness the clear husks,
the bell jars slipped around the bark,
so that, if a pair of mammalian eyes happened
to catch this catching of light by the fallen world,
each branch would be seen in outline, before the current

of white, like a sparkler on the Fourth, forgot
its path, or the hand that guided it forgot,
though there were no hands there, and one was left
after the fact with what light there was before,
which was none, or so little it might as well have been.

7.

By the time I'd gotten the photo
I'd almost given myself frostbite, my right hand
bee-sting red, numb, then (back

in the glove) furious.

To punish myself, I could lose a hand.
Could wear forever these glasses
frosted with breath that make every stoplight a supernova.

Ring inside ring inside ring. And at the center?

8.

I was trying to talk to her over the DJ's throb, loping
and trying not to fall.

I'd already ripped my pants
and couldn't afford a concussion. I'd seen,

I said, too many comments
on news articles where my fellow citizens
said they wished they could shoot me

in another war that we'd have, in virtue
of the meaning of words, to call civil.

I see, she said. If she heard me. I thought again
about the photo I'd wanted to take
since I saw it on the drive there.

9.

And if someone, someone who had business
        being there, thought an orange car in a soybean field

conspicuous, it being a night in January,
        the field a slab of alabaster, of white marble, of bleached quartz,

and came nearer with the thin limbs of their headlights,
        then with their arms, their body with its head, the head

with its eyes, and saw me, prone—what then?

10.

Streetlight over a tree of ice.
Silver crescents nested in shockwaves, scratched
glass against the charcoal dark.

        You could make a print of that shot so black
no one would be able to say what it was.
Photograph from the throat of a well. Cobwebs.
Someone's cursive; an angel opening its one good eye.

A vessel in spacetime. A body in a field, aglow.

Something you know you know the name for
when it sees you.

Steven Espada Dawson
Salvation Sonnet

Almost sweetly the judge gaveled away my summer,
knocking her desk lightly like a quiet neighbor's door.

I worked three hundred hours at a Salvation Army—
their motto *Blood and Fire*. Our small misfit militia,

teenagers unearthing ourselves from the stacks
of stuff left behind, piecemeal Lego sets, doll houses

with missing balconies. Some people would donate
anything for a write-off: prosthetic limbs, uncle's ashes

mistaken for a daisy vase, countless dildos, dildoes, dildi.
I learned the Spanish word—*consolador*, from *to console*.

We took fishing pictures with the biggest and brightest,
threw them in a box we hid from management like a pile

of armless crosses. When I cup my ear towards that
summer, I can sometimes hear them shiver back to life.

—Nominated by *The Adroit Journal*

Desiree C. Bailey
Orfeu Negro / Black Orpheus

—*after Marcel Camus's 1959 film*

poor blacks   sweet blacks   molasses-smeared and sticky blacks
blacks in favela erect   hoisted high in scorched hills   blacks in blue
in white   in yellow dresses   blacks yielding kites to the wind   serene
blacks   toothless blacks   beige brown black blacks   blacks nested
in hammocks being tropical blacks   blacks hawking squid and onions
hustlin blacks   cans of oil on their heads blacks   blacks summoning
sun from sea   slit-throat rooster blacks   blacks hazed in lust in lazy heat
dust blacks   spiced blacks   watermelon blacks   water dog sailor blacks
blacks whirling gold thread for carnaval   starfall blacks   star-crossed blacks
blacks busting through bas relief bossa nova blacks   glistening blacks
masked blacks   blacks in pretty painted shacks   crucifix blacks
nightfall blacks   shadow blacks   tristeza the sadness
so sweet it rots black

*

I too from masquerade land. Asphalt sputtering, chomping on plastic beads
and feathers, costumes re-singing histories of the flesh. My island a speck, a
globe of spit slipping past the eye of the world. So I watch *Orfeu Negro* greedy
for a glimpse of myself, a skip trick of light splayed out on the screen. My
greed, my open mouth cares not for taste. I am almost ashamed. I want to be
looked upon as the world looks upon Eurydice. Delicate, the way her pistil
sways in the breeze.

O thirst of commerce, ever-sucking despite force of flow, pitching our flesh
from port to port. Aren't we charmed and exquisite, dancing as we've always
danced, drenched in our cane-taint?

*

Swig of dawn, orchid's exhale
hounds the cliff. Camera's invitation: see

the bodies framed by fronds of paradise. No space
for my mourning. The dirge is drowned in the bay.

Children twist limbs
to dance, hoisting the sun
with guitar strings.

No space for my—.

Orfeu gone. Eurydice dissolved
in the plucked refrain.
Where a black falls, another

dances up from the soil. Happy blacks, cycle
of blacks, kicking up dust.

—Nominated by the New York University
Creative Writing Program

Courtney Faye Taylor
Grief for the Horizontal World

Everything that I've ever done
I keep in a jar marked *innocent*
so that men can't touch it.

Most flies tire of gossip
they've prayed to be on the wall of.
They roll such funky eyes, yawning

over grownfolks' most beautiful
business. I sit with hands tied in a lie
behind my own ass, a patient

afro donkey. I am the only trick alive
and with eyes who likes outgrown
acrylics and who likes it when

wind blows a water fountain's show
onto a sidewalk in a park the size
of Portugal. I think, *boss confetti*. Yesterday

I am twenty-six and the home
you will rape me in has not been
built yet. Catching my fat reflection

in an hourglass, I don't seem capable
of creating what I have: a fear with proportions
the size of disaster. Portugal and disaster

are the exact same size for me. My fear
is a park and inside of her a water
fountain blows its show onto

styrofoam boardwalks. The home
she'll find me trippin' in has not
been built, yet it's gorgeous and owned

by men who touch jars
marked *capable*. I know facts about
Grecian Troy and one popular myth

about Trojans: *If u carry one,
u won't need it. If u leave it,
u'll seem clean or*

childishly kind.   I kill a fly minding its business
on a sidewalk inside of me today. Why?   I know I'll enjoy
the music. As a mother of something black

I owe flies nothing.   Nothing. I owe
nothing.   Remember that.

Rob Colgate
Chicken Skewer

I reenter my body as a crab until I realize that a crab
means nothing to me, so I reenter as a lobster,
which ends up being more of the same, and then
his pinchers stop pinching and start holding
back his tears like marbles in a vase.
Outside of my body there is a flock of birds
pecking sapphires out of the sidewalk. They don't fly
away when I approach but they do start
shouting names—Mateo! Doug! Graham!
Can't you see this body is yours,
crumpled on the closet mattress after
too much at Skylark. Too much at Currier,
flipping upside down and down
until the direction enters my body and says, OK,
I'll be your boyfriend, you can hold my hand,
but only when we are in different zipcodes and I've had
too much at Scarlet. I promise to keep my flock very small.
We're just trying this out, chicken and a nickel, video of us
in Times Square, getting eggs from the store
and filling the canvas bag with museums
because we forgot about the eggs.
Michael forgets to say goodnight to me,
and as luck would have it, it's the night
that my duvet cracks open and all of the cicadas pour out,
start tossing bits of my brain back and forth.
Thomas, you could've stopped this!
I reenter my body as all of the oranges in the wooden crate
propped up on 82nd and Amsterdam. It isn't Amsterdam

without Finn screaming down the afternoon
because he's supposed to be home by now.
Listen, you're already home, but you won't know it
until the boy holding the coffee starts to pack your suitcase
underneath the stairs. And even your sister can't stop
crying now, salt chalking up the tires of the bus—
I reenter my body as a highway, then a Monday, then a demo
of a pop song that never made it to the surface.
I reenter this room as someone who doesn't know how
cancer actually causes death but cries
when he thinks about Max and Tim.
And now there's more crying in this room, reentering
as a presymptomatic blip, Kevin as a movie
and Kevin as a chunk of sapphire who hates
watching movies, who drowns during the previews.
And I am very lonely, haven't felt together in hours now,
several thousand really. In January I took a weekend trip
to visit my circumstances, gutter slush and blond boys.
I got a stack of pancakes out of the whole ordeal, but then
the pancakes tried to reenter my body
as tickets to a play, and then as a book. Not sure
how much either cost. I've been pretty distracted
since I started trying to reenter my body as a coffee mug.
The mug is full, if you know what I mean—
I mean that I still love you, Brandon,
and all my dripping bones and pissy legs and fuzzy eyes
were just ways to zip you up in an Alan-sized wrapper (Alan,
I love you too). We used to do this thing
where we would make an empire and forget
what we were the emperors of. Everyone wants to follow us
but no one will kiss the door. The pinch reenters my body
as cracked eggshells on the ground.

Leyla Çolpan
Daughter Conditionals, or If Winters Were of Two Kinds

The kind which whitens the earth
and the kind which widens it—

If the winter were precious
        for its whiteness   If whiteness

were a pearl sown in the under-ash
        of my maternal line   strung out

along its daughters' white thread—
        the queer grey hazel   rooting

in our new country   a new
        Kuşköy, an American Giresun

If winter were the opal
        film across grandmother's hazel

eyes—If winter were precious
        for her blindness   If I were

precious were the pearl were the
        You   who could subsist in the ice

of this country, mother, walk it whole
        in whiteness,   the You dilute

enough for West Virginia   widened
        If winter were a gift you

fashioned from my father's bones
        If your daughter were precious

with his whiteness   If whiteness
        let her speak your mother's tongue

uncleaved   If winter widened
        in the timbers of our house come

frost—If it cast roof tiles through white arms
        of Appalachian birch
            like tinsel

I would instill   the hazel
        fissures of your face in mine

would still gather up your hair, laid
        dark and precious as the earth.

Jim Whiteside
Clock with Reverse Gears

I'm ten and jumping
out of the pool

onto the concrete, wet
only with sweat, walking

back to the machine
that reassembles the lawn

one blade at a time.
Birds call out with songs

that quickly retreat
to their lungs.

Your body is made
whole again, the flames

returning flesh to bone.
I have a father

and then, suddenly,
I don't. This is

the part that doesn't
change back.

In the field where
we bury you,

the bag with your ashes
never empties—

the hole overflows
while I stand there

waiting for your voice
to come through

the wind. Every fish
you ever caught

re-embodies, spits out
the bait and swims

away, while I sit
in a dark room

wearing your bathrobe,
watching your hand

reaching around
the doorframe

to switch the light off
and on, off and on,

until the bulb blows out.

Mary Block
After Rebmann and the Safari Collection Brochure

Like a bird in a restaurant
I've been transformed
by the walls around me
into a filthy thing,
a hovering problem
who moves too fast
and doesn't know how to leave.

Like the ten-foot alligator caught
in a Clearwater kitchen,
hissing and thrashing around
in a puddle of red wine and glass,
I've been monstrously wrong.
My fury's gone viral.
My body's been made absurd
for its size and its suffering,
made available to subscribers.

Like the herd of giraffes
with their heads
through a hotel window
I want my beauty back.
I want to understand my rights
on either side of a given partition.
If a window implies permission,
turns me into the freaky background
of someone else's vacation photos
I want to know
before I let myself get too close.

Mark Kyungsoo Bias
And Now That I'm Done, I Give Him Back to You

//

Preserving what was severed, the brain goes over-
looked.

Each morning, it brings the dust into this home, has me
tamper

with the clockwork. The winter sets back another
hour.

//

I distort the image. I blame the weather.

//

When the bathroom door was ajar, I thought it a miniature landscape.
A circular figure dangling from an extension chord.

A hand making incisions.
A bare thigh filling a bathtub.

//

I'm giving you this page because I don't know what to do
with it. Love was always a wire dipping into water.

//

Don't you know
what I'm capable of
by now?

New gods were built
out of fear.

Because no one was
coming to fill what
I knew as silence.
What I now know as
the pinhole of my being.

//

The balance shifts.

      We can survive this night. But we're never done.

//

          Days moved through the window
      before the baby came out
      biting. Keeping its arms
              at its sides, the hardest task was to relax
                    the tongue.

//

Here is the lock. Here are the keys to my eyelids.

//

When the sky broke and flooded,
the machine stopped blinking.
We heard the children calling
just across the street. We saw it all
and still, no answer. No way to beg-
in. No language to pardon our mouths for spilling.

//

I'm convinced it was a trick
to bring me to the table. Confessing everything until
everything was capsuled in a golden moon.

//

Something grew legs to keep up when I was leaving.

All my life, I was chased down by a dwindling voice.

        the voice saying, please. you're only a dog off his leash.

—Nominated by UMass Amherst
MFA for Poets and Writers

Benjamin Goldberg
Dog-Head's Creation Story

I swung a hammer once.
A boy wandered to the center
of his lawn, and knelt. He carried
a plastic bag. He dragged
a leather leash. This was night.
I haven't touched a hammer since.
He cradled the empty leash,
then fell. I didn't strike. He beheld
the jaws of the animal I made
for him, and his whole life
he'd mistake it for the sky—
its solitary yellow eye, the nail
where I'd hung my name.
I won't explain. It was hard to see.
I haven't held a hammer since.
Once, I almost tried to speak.
These aren't stars. They're teeth.

Colby Cotton
Devotional

How many nights I've seen You in the machinery
of a dog, tracking the scent
of squirrels through the pines. How many

nights I've felt the clicking die
in the mind of a mouse, and blanketed in frost—
have I walked the stone road

the half-mile to the bright barn, and felt figureless
in the wheat. You have never asked me
to live in the streams, and would never let me

stay young in the irises.
You would probe the brain of an ox
chewing cattails and its cud. You would enter

the brain of anyone who believes
he has discovered a new genus of flower
as I ebbed out on the floor in a dream. Each night

I wake dry-mouthed by the black hall,
opening a spigot. At the end
of the hour, as You bore down this tunnel

of sleep, I feel my ghost kneel at the spigots—
I put my hand through my head
trying to place You there.

Dujie Tahat
Salat to Be Read from Right to Left

Helal Marwa after—

[adhan]

messages Facebook me sends uncle My
does translator Facebook .understand barely I
. ح with starts One .images to apply not

.amo ,you love I writes He

[standing]

,clothes Friday my In
skips he as me sees homie the
just is mosque The .school
from corner the round house a
.algebra period second

[bowing]

phone my over Hovering
7abibi why searching I'm
name pop's if as—habibi not and
.line the on weren't

[prostration]

.Rayan Al Dujanaht it's ,God of house wooden this In
even sometimes ,gate the at ,Dujie

different is father my ,Here .way the on
course Of .same the or
wild this ,prayer all it's

pushing ,corner the to jockeying
.another down back then ,out not up

[again prostration]

?this say to How

[sitting]

*.God by Confounded

[alaikum salam]

direction which days these note I
foot what ,drip ablution of drops last the
,shoes my on back putting when first goes
.shut slams gate the how

———————
الحمدلله *

Kaveh Bassiri
Homecoming

When everyone has gone, while the clouds still
argue loud with the stars, I sit near him,
wipe his shoulders, dip my hand in the small
of his back, unbutton the pump, the drainage.
I unwrap the blue robe, like candy. Scent
of moldered covers pours on the floor, I
rise over my father, lunate, plant bulbs
in his eye sockets, winnow heart from lungs.

I groom him for Shahrazad, who's waiting.
Irises, tulips are sprouting. Patiently
holding to his spine, I shake the branches,
pluck arms, legs, the tongue, his penis. I lift
his chest; the latches fall as I open
the shutters. Splayed, his pelvis fills with leaves.

—Nominated by *Shenandoah*

Acknowledgments

Threa Almontaser's "Hidden Bombs in My Coochie" previously appeared in *Passages North*.

Aldo Amparán's "Thanatophobia" previously appeared in *Fugue*.

Jasmine An's "Sports Science" previously appeared in *Black Warrior Review*'s *Boyfriend Village*.

Kathleen Balma's "Lap Dance with No Ending" previously appeared in *New Ohio Review*.

Daniel Barnum's "Would I Change All I Know for Unknowing" previously appeared in *Muzzle Magazine*.

Caroline Parkman Barr's "For Some Time After" previously appeared in *South Carolina Review*.

Kaveh Bassiri's "Homecoming" previously appeared in *Shenandoah*.

Rob Colgate's "Chicken Skewer" previously appeared in *The Margins*.

Leyla Çolpan's "Daughter Conditionals, or If Winters Were of Two Kinds" previously appeared in *Frontier Poetry*.

Michaela Coplen's "Gate Control" previously appeared in *GASHER*.

Colby Cotton's "Devotional" previously appeared in *Bennington Review*.

Imani Davis's "Everything Must Go" previously appeared in *The Adroit Journal*.

Steven Espada Dawson's "Salvation Sonnet" previously appeared in
The Adroit Journal.

Jai Dulani's "My Name" previously appeared in *Waxwing*.

Sara Elkamel's "Field of No Justice" previously appeared in
Four Way Review.

Benjamin Garcia's "Huitlacoche" previously appeared in *Palette Poetry*.

torrin a. greathouse's "Abecedarian Requiring Further Examination Before
a Diagnosis Can Be Determined" previously appeared in *Poetry*.

Zach Linge's "Fingers on a Gay Man" previously appeared in *Poetry*.

Erin Marie Lynch's "St. Helens" previously appeared in *Narrative*.

Thomas McGuire's "Four Ways of Looking at Magpie—A Most
Becoming Bird" previously appeared in *Poetics for the
More-Than-Human World*.

Jae Nichelle's "Three Churches Burn in Louisiana" previously appeared
in *Washington Square Review*.

Catherine Pond's "Forest Horse" previously appeared in *Narrative*.

Paige Quiñones's "Aubade" previously appeared in *The Adroit Journal*.

Cintia Santana's "REIGN" previously appeared in *Kenyon Review Online*.

Simon Shieh's "Kindness Comes Too Easily to Wicked Men" previously
appeared in *Passages North*.

Sophia Stid's "Apophatic Ghazal" previously appeared in *Witness*.

Dujie Tahat's "Salat to Be Read from Right to Left" previously appeared in *Poetry*.

Courtney Faye Taylor's "Grief for the Horizontal World" previously appeared in *The Adroit Journal*.

Michael Torres's "All-American Mexican" previously appeared in *Southern Humanities Review*.

Tasia Trevino's "The Other Side of Mt. Heart Attack" previously appeared in *The Account*.

Jesús I. Valles's "Gatorade, pepino y limon" previously appeared in *The McNeese Review*.

Troy Varvel's "Complete" previously appeared in *Dialogist*.

Michael M. Weinstein's "Anniversary" previously appeared on the Academy of American Poets website.

Jim Whiteside's "Clock with Reverse Gears" previously appeared in *Sycamore Review*.

Jameka Williams's "My Sister Says [Everyone Can Catch This Smoke]" previously appeared in *Oyez Review*.

Alicia Wright's "Everything That Rises" previously appeared in *The Paris Review*.

Jessica Yuan's "Disorientation" previously appeared in *Tahoma Literary Review*.

Contributors' Notes

THREA ALMONTASER is the author of the forthcoming poetry collection *The Wild Fox of Yemen* (Graywolf Press, 2021), selected by Harryette Mullen for the 2020 Walt Whitman Award from The Academy of American Poets. She teaches English to immigrants and refugees in Raleigh. For more, please visit threawrites.com.

ALDO AMPARÁN is a queer, Mexican American poet from the border/cities of El Paso, Texas, and Ciudad Juárez, Chihuahua, Mexico. He is the author of *Brother Sleep* (Alice James Books, 2022), winner of the 2020 Alice James Award. A CantoMundo Fellow, his work has appeared in *AGNI*, *Gulf Coast*, *The Journal*, *Kenyon Review Online*, *Poetry Northwest*, and elsewhere. He earned his MFA from the University of Texas at El Paso. Find him online at aldoamparan.com.

JASMINE AN comes from the Midwest. Her work exists in *Black Warrior Review*, *Nat. Brut*, and *Waxwing*, among others, and two chapbooks: *Naming the No-Name Woman* (Two Sylvias Press, 2016) and *Monkey Was Here* (Porkbelly Press, 2020).

DESIREE C. BAILEY is the author of *What Noise Against the Cane* (Yale University Press, 2021), selected by Carl Phillips as the winner of the 2020 Yale Series of Younger Poets. She is also the author of the fiction chapbook *In Dirt or Saltwater* (O'clock Press, 2016) and has been published in the *Academy of American Poets* website, *Best American Poetry*, and *Callaloo*, among other publications. Desiree has an MFA in fiction from Brown University and is an MFA poetry candidate at New York University. Born in Trinidad and Tobago, Desiree grew up in Queens, New York, and is currently an English teacher in Brooklyn.

KATHLEEN BALMA is a teacher, librarian, and veteran of the U.S. Navy. Her awards include a Fulbright teaching grant, a Pushcart Prize, scholarships from the Bread Loaf Environmental Writers' Conference and Sewanee Writers' Conference, and a writer-in-residence fellowship from Rivendell Writers' Colony. She grew up in the Ohio River Valley of Illinois and has lived in the Ozarks, Andalucía, New South Wales, Western Australia, New England, Castilla la Mancha, and several corners of the American Midwest. She makes her home in New Orleans.

DANIEL BARNUM grew up in New England and now lives and writes in Columbus, Ohio. A former fellow at the Bucknell Seminar for Undergraduate Poets, they currently serve as the managing editor of *The Journal.* Their poems and essays appear in or are forthcoming from *West Branch, Hayden's Ferry Review, The Massachusetts Review, The Offing, Pleiades,* and elsewhere. *Names for Animals,* their debut chapbook, was selected for the Robin Becker Prize from Seven Kitchens Press and published in March 2020. More at danielbarnum.net

CAROLINE PARKMAN BARR is a recent graduate of the MFA Writing Program at the University of North Carolina at Greensboro, where she served as poetry editor of *The Greensboro Review.* Her poetry appears or is forthcoming in *The Pinch, RHINO, South Carolina Review, NELLE, Connotation Press,* and elsewhere. She is currently an editorial assistant for *Poetry Northwest* and living in Birmingham, Alabama.

KAVEH BASSIRI is the author of two chapbooks: *99 Names of Exile,* the winner of the Anzaldúa Poetry Prize (2018), and *Elementary English,* the winner of Rick Campbell Chapbook Prize (2020). His poems have been published in *Best American Poetry 2020, Best New Poets 2011, Verse Daily, Virginia Quarterly Review, Copper Nickel, Beloit Poetry Journal, The Cincinnati Review,* and *TYPO.* He is also the recipient of a 2019 translation fellowship from the National Endowment for the Arts. His translations have appeared in *The Common, Denver Quarterly, Chicago Review, The Massachusetts Review, The Los Angeles Review, Guernica,* and *Colorado Review.*

MARK KYUNGSOO BIAS is a Korean American poet and a recipient of the 2020 William Matthews Poetry Prize. His work has appeared or is forthcoming in *Asheville Poetry Review*, *IDK Magazine*, *PANK*, and elsewhere. The Saejowi Initiative for National Integration, which seeks to provide aid to North Korean refugees, has also featured his work. He is a consultant at Grub Street, an instructor at the Juniper Institute for Young Writers, and an MFA candidate at the University of Massachusetts Amherst.

MARY BLOCK is a Miami-born, Miami-based poet. Her work has appeared in *RHINO*, *Sonora Review*, *Nimrod International Journal*, and others. Her poems can be found online at *Rattle*, *SWWIM Every Day*, and *Aquifer: The Florida Review Online*. Mary is a graduate of NYU's Creative Writing Program, a Best of the Net finalist, a Ruth Lilly Fellowship finalist, and a Pushcart Prize nominee. More at maryblock.net

RACHEL BUSNARDO holds an MFA from the University of Colorado at Boulder. Her work can be found in *DIAGRAM*, *Bone Bouquet*, *So Say We All*, *DREGINALD*, and elsewhere. She currently lives and works in Colorado.

ROB COLGATE is a poet and educator from Evanston, Illinois. He holds a degree in psychology from Yale University and studied at the Iowa Writers' Workshop during the summer of 2019. He currently attends the New Writers Project at UT Austin, where he is pursuing his MFA in poetry alongside a certificate in critical disability studies. In Austin, he teaches creative writing workshops through The Library Foundation's Badgerdog program and serves as the nonfiction editor for *Bat City Review*. His work appears in *Salt Hill*, *The Margins*, and *Voicemail Poems*, among others. His first chapbook, *So Dark the Gap*, was published by Tammy in March 2020. You can find him at robcolgate.com.

ANDREW COLLARD is a PhD student and instructor at Western Michigan University. His poems have appeared in *Ploughshares*, *Crazyhorse*, and

AGNI, among other journals. Originally from southeast Michigan, he currently lives in Grand Rapids.

LEYLA ÇOLPAN is the author of *What Passes & What Passes Through* (Ghost City Press, 2020), a collaborative chapbook with artist Sasha Barile in benefit of Southside Harm Reduction Services of Minneapolis. Ze was an inaugural Creative Arts Fellow at the University of Pittsburgh, where ze was awarded an Academy of American Poets Undergraduate Prize for hir work on assimilation, multiethnicity, and bilinguality. Ze is the winner of the 2020 Gulf Coast Prize for Poetry, judged by Kazim Ali, and hir poetry and essays have recently appeared in *The Adroit Journal*, *Columbia Journal*, and *Homology Lit*. Readers can follow hir work on Twitter @ LeylaColpan.

MICHAELA COPLEN is a doctoral candidate at the University of Oxford. Her poems have been published online with *The Atlantic* and poets.org, as well as in print with the *Bellevue Literary Review* and in *Here: Poems for the Planet*. She has been a National Student Poet, a Bucknell Seminar fellow, and won the 2019 Troubadour International Poetry Prize. Her work can found at michaelacoplen.com.

COLBY COTTON is from a small town in western New York. A 2018–2020 Wallace Stegner Fellow at Stanford, he is a graduate of the MFA Writing Program at The University of North Carolina at Greensboro and a recipient of a Tennessee Williams Scholarship from the Sewanee Writers' Conference. His work appears or is forthcoming in the *Missouri Review*, *Prairie Schooner*, *Cincinnati Review*, *Alaska Quarterly Review*, and *32 Poems*, among others. He lives in Oakland, California.

IMANI DAVIS is a queer Black writer from Brooklyn. Their poems have recently appeared with *PBS Newshour's Brief But Spectacular Series*, Best of the Net, *The Offing*, Shade Literary Arts, and *The Adroit Journal*. A Mellon-Mays Fellow, they've also earned fellowships from Lambda Literary, BOAAT Press, and the Stadler Center. They hold a BA in

English and Africana Studies from the University of Pennsylvania, and are currently a doctoral student in American Studies at Harvard. They're twenty-one. For more, visit imani-davis.com.

STEVEN ESPADA DAWSON is a writer from East Los Angeles by way of Denver. The son of a Mexican immigrant, his poems have appeared recently in *The Adroit Journal, New Ohio Review, Thrush*, and *Hobart*. He tweets @verylargemoth.

JAI DULANI is a poet, writer, and multimedia artist who spent most of his life in New York City by way of Pittsburgh, Pennsylvania, and Chandigarh, India. His poetry and nonfiction have appeared in or are forthcoming in *The Offing, Foglifter, Waxwing, No Tokens, Porcupine Literary, Golden Walkman Magazine* and elsewhere. His articles have appeared in *Open City* and *Teachers & Writers Magazine*. He has received fellowships from Kundiman, VONA/Voices, and the Asian American Writers' Workshop. Dulani holds an MFA in creative writing from Western Washington University, where he served as the 2019–2020 assistant managing editor of the *Bellingham Review*. He is co-editor of the anthology, *The Revolution Starts At Home: Confronting Intimate Violence in Activist Communities*.

SARA ELKAMEL is a poet and journalist living between her hometown, Cairo, and New York City. She holds an MA in arts journalism from Columbia University and is currently an MFA candidate in poetry at New York University. Named a 2020 Gregory Djanikian Scholar by *The Adroit Journal*, Elkamel has had poems appear in *The Common, Michigan Quarterly Review, The Rumpus, Nimrod International Journal, Four Way Review, The Boiler, American Chordata*, and as part of the anthologies *Halal If You Hear Me* and *20.35 Africa*, among other publications.

LIZA FLUM's poems have appeared in *Narrative, The Tampa Review, The Southeast Review, Lambda Literary*, and *Zócalo Public Square*. She is a recipient of a Barbara Deming individual artist grant, and her writing has been supported by fellowships from the Saltonstall Foundation, the Vermont Studio Center, the Kimmel Harding Nelson Center and Aspen Summer Words. She holds an MFA in poetry from Cornell, and she is currently a PhD candidate in literature and creative writing at the University of Utah where she is a Francois Camoin Fellow. She works as a poetry editor for Omnidawn Publishing.

BENJAMIN GARCIA's first collection, *Thrown in the Throat* (Milkweed Editions, August 2020), was selected by Kazim Ali for the 2019 National Poetry Series. He works as a sexual health and harm reduction educator throughout the Finger Lakes region of New York. His poems have recently appeared or are forthcoming in *AGNI*, *American Poetry Review*, *Kenyon Review*, and *New England Review*. He will be joining the inaugural faculty at Alma College's low-residency MFA Program in 2021. Find him online at benjamingarciapoet.com.

BENJAMIN GOLDBERG received an MFA from Johns Hopkins University. His poems have appeared or are forthcoming in *Poetry*, *TriQuarterly*, *West Branch*, *Blackbird*, *Verse Daily*, *Best New Poets 2014*, and elsewhere. He lives with his wife outside Washington, D.C. Find him online at benrgold.com.

TORRIN A. GREATHOUSE is a trans poet, cripple-punk, and MFA candidate at the University of Minnesota. Her work is published in *Ploughshares*, *New England Review*, *TriQuarterly*, and *The Kenyon Review*. She is the author of *Wound from the Mouth of a Wound* (Milkweed Editions, 2020).

JACKSON HOLBERT was born and raised in eastern Washington and currently lives in Texas. His work has been published in *Field*, *Narrative*, and *The Nation*. He has received fellowships from The Michener Center for Writers and The Stadler Center for Poetry and has been a finalist for a Ruth Lilly and Dorothy Sargent Rosenberg Fellowship.

ANDREW DAVID KING is from California. A graduate of the Iowa Writers' Workshop, he was 2019–2020 Provost's Visiting Writer and Visiting Assistant Professor in the University of Iowa's Department of English, where he co-founded *Diptych: A Book Artists' and Writers' Reading Series*. His writing and art appear in *Best New Poets 2018*, *ZYZZYVA*, *Poetry*, *Crab Orchard Review*, *Parenthesis*, and other places, including *A Field Guide to the Poetry of Theodore Roethke* (Ohio University Press/Swallow Press, 2020). When he isn't walking the oak and redwood forests of the coast, he's thinking about it.

ZACH LINGE's poems appear in *AGNI*, *New England Review*, *Poetry*, and elsewhere. Linge is the recipient of scholarships to The Kenyon Review Writers Workshop and the Sewanee Writers' Conference, and lives in Tallahassee, where they serve as editor-in-chief of the *Southeast Review* and teach poetry. Follow them on Twitter @ZachLinge or see more work at zachlinge.com.

CAMERON QUAN LOUIE lives in Tucson, where he serves on the board of directors with poetry nonprofit POG. He received his MFA in creative writing from the University of Washington in Seattle. He was a 2019 grant recipient from the Arts Foundation of Tucson and Southern Arizona, and in 2016 he was a Multiplying Mediums Fellow. You can find his recent poems, prose, and erasures in *jubilat*, *Sonora Review*, *Fourth Genre*, *Quarterly West*, *Entropy*, *Pacifica Literary Review*, and *The Margins*, among others. See his work and get in touch at cameronqlouie.com.

ERIN MARIE LYNCH is a poet and artist. Her writing has appeared in journals such as *New England Review*, *Gulf Coast*, *Narrative*, and *DIAGRAM*, while her performance and video work has been featured at a variety of exhibitions and festivals. Born and raised in Oregon, she is a descendant of the Standing Rock Sioux Tribe. Currently, she is a PhD student in creative writing and literature at the University of Southern California.

THOMAS MCGUIRE is a poet, translator, essayist, and Irish Studies scholar. His creative work has appeared in *North American Review, Poetry for The More-Than-Human-World: An Anthology of Poetry & Commentary, Southeast Review, Dispatches from the Poetry Wars,* and *Open-Eyed, Full-Throated: An Anthology of American/Irish Poets.* An associate professor at the U.S. Air Force Academy in Colorado, he also serves as poetry editor for *War, Literature & the Arts.* In 2008 he was a Fulbright Scholar to Ireland. He lives with his wife and children in the rain shadow of Pike's Peak where he frequently writes about magpies, the Arkansas River watershed, and Native American culturally modified trees. Contact him at thomas. mcguire@afacademy.af.edu

CARLING MCMANUS is an artist, writer, and entrepreneur working in Appalachia. She holds an MFA from the San Francisco Art Institute and a BA in religious studies from McGill University. She has poetry forthcoming in the *Beloit Poetry Journal.* Carling lives on a mountainside with her wife and two border collies in Mink Shoals, West Virginia. Find her online at carlingmcmanus.com.

KELLY MCQUAIN is the author of *Velvet Rodeo,* which won the Bloom chapbook poetry prize. His prose, poetry, and illustrations have appeared in *The Pinch, Painted Bride Quarterly, The Philadelphia Inquirer, Rogue Agent, Spunk, Assaracus,* and *Cleaver,* as well as such anthologies as *The Queer South, Drawn to Marvel, LGBTQ Fiction and Poetry from Appalachia, Eyes Glowing at the Edge of the Woods: Fiction and Poetry from West Virginia,* and *Rabbit Ears: TV Poems.* As a visual artist, McQuain has won prizes from the Barnes Foundation and the William Way LGBTQ Center, and his series of writer portraits appear as cover illustrations at *Fjords Review.* He has been a Sewanee Tennessee Williams Scholar and a Lambda Literary Fellow, and he has received two fellowships from the Pennsylvania Council on the Arts. For more, see KellyMcQuain.wordpress.com.

ISABEL RIES NEAL is a Zell Fellow in poetry at the University of Michigan. She has been awarded fellowships by the Provincetown Fine Arts Work

Center, Haystack Mountain School of Crafts, the Vermont Studio Center, and the Yiddish Book Center. She lives and works in Chicago.

JAE NICHELLE is one of the few people from Lafayette, Louisiana, who has never met the singer Cupid. Her work has appeared in *The Offing Magazine, Muzzle Magazine, Vinyl Poetry and Prose, ColorBloq Magazine*, and elsewhere. You can find some of her other musings at jaenichelle.com.

CATHERINE POND is the author of *Fieldglass* (SIU Press, 2021). Her poems have appeared in *Best American Nonrequired Reading, Narrative Magazine, The Adroit Journal, AGNI*, and other publications. She has received fellowships from the University of Southern California, the New York State Summer Writers Institute, and the James Merrill House. Pond lives in California, where she is a PhD candidate in creative writing at USC.

PAIGE QUIÑONES's work has appeared or is forthcoming in *The Adroit Journal, Copper Nickel, Crazyhorse, Juked, Lambda Literary, Orion Magazine, Poetry Northwest, Quarterly West, Sixth Finch*, and elsewhere. She earned her MFA from the Ohio State University and is currently a PhD student in poetry at the University of Houston, where she serves as a poetry editor for *Gulf Coast*. Her first poetry collection, *The Best Prey*, won the Lena-Miles Wever Todd Prize at Pleiades Press and is forthcoming in February 2021.

CINTIA SANTANA is a poet, translator, and interdisciplinary artist. Her work has appeared in *Beloit Poetry Journal, Gulf Coast, Harvard Review, The Iowa Review, Kenyon Review, Michigan Quarterly Review, The Missouri Review, Narrative, Pleiades, Poetry Northwest, The Threepenny Review, West Branch*, and other journals. The recipient of fellowships from CantoMundo and the Djerassi Resident Artists Program, she teaches poetry and fiction workshops in Spanish, as well as literary translation courses, at Stanford University. Learn more at cintiasantana.com.

JOHANN SARNA is originally from Toronto, Canada. He now lives in Austin, where he recently received an MFA from the University of Texas. His poems have appeared in *Narrative* and *Ninth Letter*.

SIMON SHIEH is a poet, essayist, and educator living in Beijing. A lifelong martial artist, Simon competed in his first professional Muay Thai fight at seventeen years old in Shanghai. The day before he turned twenty-one, Simon suffered his first and only loss by knockout in Brazil. Soon after, he turned away from fighting and found poetry. The work of Jericho Brown, Eduardo Corral, Louise Glück, Terrance Hayes, Ocean Vuong, Lucie Brock-Broido, and many others opened the doors for his poems. A full list of Simon's publications can be found at simonshieh.com.

SOPHIA STID is a poet from California. She is the 2019–2021 Ecotone Postgraduate Fellow at UNC Wilmington, where she teaches creative writing and edits for *Ecotone*. She earned her MFA from Vanderbilt University in 2019 and has received fellowships from the Bucknell Seminar for Younger Poets, the Sewanee Writers' Conference, and the Collegeville Institute. She is the winner of the 2017 Francine Ringold Award for New Writers and the 2019 Witness Literary Award in Poetry. Recent poems and essays can be found in *Image, Pleiades, Ninth Letter, Hayden's Ferry Review*, and *The Cincinnati Review*. Her website is sophiastid.com.

DUJIE TAHAT is a Filipino-Jordanian immigrant living in Washington state. They are the author of *Here I Am O My God*, selected by Fady Joudah for a Poetry Society of America Chapbook Fellowship, and *Salat*, selected by Cornelius Eady as winner of the Tupelo Press Sunken Garden Chapbook Award. Along with Luther Hughes and Gabrielle Bates, they cohost *The Poet Salon* podcast.

COURTNEY FAYE TAYLOR is a graduate of Agnes Scott College and the University of Michigan Helen Zell Writers' Program. She is the winner of the 92Y Discovery/Boston Review Poetry Prize and an Academy of American Poets Prize. Her work appears in *Ploughshares*, *Kenyon Review*, *The Adroit Journal*, *TriQuarterly*, *Witness*, and elsewhere. Courtney is the poetry editor of *SLICE Magazine*. Find her online at courtneyfayetaylor.com.

MICHAEL TORRES was born and brought up in Pomona, California, where he spent his adolescence as a graffiti artist. His debut collection of poems, *An Incomplete List of Names* (Beacon Press, Oct. 2020), was selected by Raquel Salas Rivera for the National Poetry Series. His honors include awards and support from the National Endowment for the Arts, the McKnight Foundation, the Bread Loaf Writers' Conference, CantoMundo, VONA Voices, the Minnesota State Arts Board, the Jerome Foundation, the Camargo Foundation, and the Loft Literary Center. Currently he's an assistant professor in the MFA program at Minnesota State University, Mankato, and a teaching artist with the Minnesota Prison Writing Workshop. Visit him at michaeltorreswriter.com.

TASIA TREVINO is a writer and musician from California. Her work has appeared in *Fence*, *PANK*, *Prelude*, *Yalobusha Review*, and more. More at tasiatrevino.com.

JESÚS I. VALLES is a queer Mexican immigrant, writer-performer from Ciudad Juárez/El Paso. Jesús' work has been supported by Lambda Literary, Sewanee Writers' Conference, Community of Writers, Idyllwild Arts, Undocupoets, *Tin House*, and the Poetry Incubator. Their work has been featured in *The New Republic*, *Quarterly West*, *The Adroit Journal*, *PANK*, NPR, and elsewhere. They are the author and performer of *(Un) Documents*, for which they earned two B. Iden Payne Awards, including Outstanding Lead Actor in a Drama and Outstanding Original Script. Jesús is currently OUTSider festival's OUTsider-in-residence.

TROY VARVEL holds an MFA from Southern Illinois University Carbondale. Runner-up in *The Missouri Review*'s 2020 Miller Audio Prize in poetry, his work has appeared or is forthcoming in *Dialogist*, *Iron Horse Literary*

Review, River Styx, storySouth, and *Yemassee,* among others. He lives and teaches in the Texas Hill Country. Find him online at troyvarvel.com.

MICHAEL M. WEINSTEIN is a trans/crip writer, researcher, and teacher. He is currently a Helen Zell Creative Writing Fellow at the University of Michigan.

JIM WHITESIDE is the author of a chapbook, *Writing Your Name on the Glass* (Bull City Press, 2019) and is a Wallace Stegner Fellow in Poetry at Stanford University. His recent poems have appeared in *Ploughshares, The Southern Review, Gulf Coast,* and *Boston Review,* among others. Originally from Cookeville, Tennessee, he holds an MFA from the University of North Carolina at Greensboro and lives in Oakland, California. Find him on Twitter at @whiteside_jim or read more of his poems at jimwhitesidepoetry.com.

JAMEKA WILLIAMS is an MFA candidate at Northwestern University hailing from Chester, Pennsylvania, fifteen miles southeast of Philadelphia. Her poetry has been published in *Prelude Magazine, Gigantic Sequins, Powder Keg Magazine, Muzzle Magazine, Yemassee, Tupelo Quarterly, Painted Bride Quarterly, Jet Fuel Review, Shrew Magazine,* and *Oyez Review.* Her poetry has been nominated for the Pushcart Prize, and is also forthcoming in New American Press's *New Poetry of the Midwest 2019–2020* anthology. She resides in Chicago, Illinois.

JESSICA YUAN is author of the chapbook *Threshold Amnesia* (2020), winner of the Yemassee Chapbook Contest. She has received fellowships from Kundiman and Miami Writer's Institute, and her poems have appeared in *jubilat, Boulevard, Ninth Letter, cream city review, River Styx, The Southampton Review, The Journal,* and elsewhere. She holds a master's in architecture from Harvard and currently lives in Boston. Her work can be found at jessicayuan.com.

Participating Magazines

32 Poems
32poems.com

3Elements Literary Review
3elementsreview.com/
   current-journal

The Account
theaccountmagazine.com

The Adroit Journal
theadroitjournal.org

AGNI Magazine
agnionline.bu.edu

American Literary Review
americanliteraryreview.com

Anomaly
anmly.org

The Antioch Review
review.antiochcollege.edu

Apple Valley Review
applevalleyreview.com

apt
apt.aforementionedproductions.com

ARTS & LETTERS
artsandletters.gcsu.edu

Atlanta Review
atlantareview.com

Atticus Review
atticusreview.org

Baty City Review
batcityreview.com

Beestung
beestungmag.com

The Believer
believermag.com

Bennington Review
benningtonreview.org

Better Than Starbucks
betterthanstarbucks.org

Birmingham Poetry Review
uab.edu/cas/englishpublications/
   birmingham-poetry-review

The Bitter Oleander
bitteroleander.com

Blackbird
blackbird.vcu.edu

Black Warrior Review
bwr.ua.edu

Blood Orange Review
bloodorangereview.com

Bloodroot
bloodrootlit.org

Boulevard
boulevardmagazine.org

Cagibi
cagibilit.com

Carve Magazine
carvezine.com

Cave Wall
cavewallpress.com

Cherry Tree
washcoll.edu/cherrytree

Cincinnati Review
cincinnatireview.com

Coal Hill Review
coalhillreview.com

The Rupture
therupturemag.com

Copper Nickel
copper-nickel.org

Crab Orchard Review
craborchardreview.siu.edu

Crazyhorse
crazyhorse.cofc.edu

cream city review
creamcityreview.org

Cumberland River Review
crr.trevecca.edu

Diode
diodepoetry.com

Ecotone
ecotonemagazine.org

EVENT Magazine
eventmagazine.ca

Fairy Tale Review
fairytalereview.com

Fjords Review
fjordsreview.com

Foglifter
foglifterjournal.com

The Georgia Review
thegeorgiareview.com

The Gettysburg Review
gettysburgreview.com

Glass: A Journal of Poetry
glass-poetry.com/journal.html

Greensboro Review
greensbororeview.org

Grist: A Journal of the Literary Arts
gristjournal.com

Guernica
guernicamag.com

Gulf Coast
gulfcoastmag.org

Hamilton Arts & Letters
HALmagazine.com

Hayden's Ferry Review
haydensferryreview.com

Hoxie Gorge Review
hoxiegorgereview.com

Image
imagejournal.org

Jet Fuel Review
jetfuelreview.com

Kenyon Review
kenyonreview.org

La Presa
embajadoraspress.com

Los Angeles Press
thelosangelespress.com

The Malahat Review
malahatreview.ca

The Margins
aaww.org

Memorious:
A Journal of New Verse & Fiction
memorious.org

Michigan Quarterly Review
sites.lsa.umich.edu/mqr

Minola Review
minolareview.com

MORIA Literary Magazine
moriaonline.com

Muzzle Magazine
muzzlemagazine.com

The Nashville Review
as.vanderbilt.edu/nashvillereview

Naugatuck River Review
naugatuckriverreview.com

New England Review
nereview.com

Newfound
newfound.org

New Ohio Review
ohio.edu/nor

New Orleans Review
neworleansreview.org

NightBlock
nightblockmag.com

Nimrod International Journal
utulsa.edu/nimrod

Okay Donkey
okaydonkeymag.com

The Los Angeles Review
losangelesreview.org

PANK
pankmagazine.com

Parentheses Journal
parenthesesjournal.com

Passages North
passagesnorth.com

Pembroke Magazine
pembrokemagazine.com

Penn Review
pennreview.org

Phoebe
phoebejournal.com

Pigeon Pages
pigeonpagesnyc.com

The Pinch
pinchjournal.com

Poet Lore
poetlore.com

Poetry
poetrymagazine.org

The Poet's Billow
thepoetsbillow.org

Porter House Review
porterhousereview.org

Posit Journal
positjournal.com

Pretty Owl Poetry
prettyowlpoetry.com

Psaltery & Lyre
psalteryandlyre.org

Puerto del Sol
puertodelsol.org

Quarterly West
quarterlywest.com

Radar Poetry
radarpoetry.com

Raleigh Review
RaleighReview.org

Rascal
rascaljournal.com

Rat's Ass Review
ratsassreview.net

Rattle
rattle.com

River Styx
riverstyx.org

Roanoke Review
roanokereview.org

Room Magazine
roommagazine.com

Ruminate Magazine
ruminatemagazine.com

Salamander
salamandermag.org

Salt Hill Review
salthilljournal.net

Sewanee Review
thesewaneereview.com

Shenandoah
shenandoahliterary.org

Slab
slablitmag.org

Slippery Elm
slipperyelm.findlay.edu

The Southeast Review
southeastreview.org

The Southern Review
thesouthernreview.org

Spillway
spillway.org

Split Lip Magazine
splitlipmagazine.com

Split Rock Review
splitrockreview.org

Sugar House Review
SugarHouseReview.com

Sundog Lit
sundoglit.com

SWWIM Every Day
swwim.org

Tahoma Literary Review
tahomaliteraryreview.com

Thrush Poetry Journal
thrushpoetryjournal.com

Tinderbox Poetry Journal
tinderboxpoetry.com

Up North Lit
upnorthlit.org

upstreet
upstreet-mag.org

Up the Staircase Quarterly
upthestaircase.org

Virginia Quarterly Review
vqronline.org

Washington Square Review
washingtonsquarereview.com

Waxwing Literary Journal
waxwingmag.org

Whale Road Review
whaleroadreview.com

wildness
readwildness.com

Participating Programs

American University Creative Writing Program
american.edu/cas/literature/mfa

Creighton University MFA in Creative Writing
creighton.edu/program/creative-writing-mfa

Florida International University MFA in Creative Writing
english.fiu.edu/creative-writing

Florida State University Creative Writing
english.fsu.edu/programs/creative-writing

Hollins University Jackson Center for Creative Writing
hollinsmfa.wordpress.com

Johns Hopkins The Writing Seminars
writingseminars.jhu.edu

Kansas State University MFA in Creative Writing Program
k-state.edu/english/programs/cw

McNeese State University MFA Program
mfa.mcneese.edu

Minnesota State University Mankato Creative Writing Program
english.mnsu.edu/cw

Monmouth University Creative Writing
monmouth.edu/school-of-humanities-social-sciences/ma-english.aspx

New Mexico State University MFA in Creative Writing
english.nmsu.edu/graduate-programs/mfa

New School Writing Program
newschool.edu/writing

New York University Creative Writing Program
as.nyu.edu/cwp

North Carolina State MFA in Creative Writing
english.chass.ncsu.edu/graduate/mfa

Northwestern University MA/MFA in Creative Writing
sps.northwestern.edu/program-areas/graduate/creative-writing

The Ohio State University MFA Program in Creative Writing
english.osu.edu/mfa

Ohio University Creative Writing PhD
ohio.edu/cas/english/grad/creative-writing/index.cfm

Pacific University Master of Fine Arts in Writing
pacificu.edu/as/mfa

Saint Mary's College of California MFA in Creative Writing
stmarys-ca.edu/mfawrite

San Diego State University MFA in Creative Writing
mfa.sdsu.edu

Syracuse University MFA in Creative Writing
english.syr.edu/cw/cw-program.html

Texas Tech University Creative Writing Program
depts.ttu.edu/english/cw

UMass Amherst MFA for Poets and Writers
umass.edu/englishmfa

UMass Boston MFA Program in Creative Writing
umb.edu/academics/cla/english/grad/mfa

UNC Greensboro Creative Writing Program
mfagreensboro.org

University of Alabama at Birmingham Graduate Theme in Creative Writing
uab.edu/cas/english/graduate-program/creative-writing

University of British Columbia Creative Writing Program
creativewriting.ubc.ca

University of Idaho MFA in Creative Writing
uidaho.edu/class/english/graduate/mfa-creative-writing

University of Illinois at Chicago Program for Writers
engl.uic.edu/CW

University of Kansas Graduate Creative Writing Program
englishcw.ku.edu

University of Maryland MFA Program
english.umd.edu

University of Memphis MFA Program
memphis.edu/english/graduate/mfa/creative_writing.php

University of Mississippi MFA in Creative Writing
mfaenglish.olemiss.edu

University of New Orleans Creative Writing Workshop
uno.edu/writing

University of North Texas Creative Writing
english.unt.edu/creative-writing-0

University of San Francisco MFA in Writing
usfca.edu/mfa

University of Southern Mississippi Center for Writers
usm.edu/english/center-writers

University of South Florida MFA in Creative Writing
english.usf.edu/graduate/concentrations/cw/degrees

University of Texas Michener Center for Writers
michener.utexas.edu

University of Utah Creative Writing Program
english.utah.edu

Vermont College of Fine Arts MFA in Writing
vcfa.edu

Virginia Tech MFA in Creative Writing Program
liberalarts.vt.edu/departments-and-schools/department-of-english/
    academic-programs/master-of-fine-arts-in-creative-writing.html

Western Michigan University Creative Writing Program
wmich.edu/english

West Virginia University MFA Program
creativewriting.wvu.edu

The series editor wishes to thank the many poets involved in our first round of reading:

Helena Chung, Kate Coleman, Andrew Eaton, Michelle Gottschlich, Emily Nason, Caleb Nolen, and Aimee Seu.

Special thanks to Jason Coleman and the University of Virginia Press for editorial advice and support.